Gift of the Nile

CHRONICLES OF ANCIENT EGYPT

Timothy R. Roberts

MetroBooks

MetroBooks

An Imprint of Friedman/Fairfax Publishers

©1999 by Michael Friedman Publishing Group, Inc.

Library of Congress Cataloging-in-Publication Data

Roberts, Timothy Roland, 1942–
    Gift of the Nile : chronicles of ancient egypt / Timothy R. Roberts
      p.   cm.
    Includes Index.
    ISBN 1-56799-585-3
    1. Egypt—History—to 332 B.C. I. Title.
    DT83.R57 1998
    932—dc21   98-22429

Editor: Celeste Sollod
Art Director: Kevin Ullrich
Designers: Milagros Sensat and Kirsten Wehmann Berger
Photography Editor: Amy Talluto
Production Manager: Camille Lee

Color separations by Bright Arts Graphics (S) Pte Ltd
Printed in Hong Kong by Sing Cheong Printing Company

10 9 8 7 6 5 4 3 2 1

For bulk purchases and special sales, please contact:
Friedman/Fairfax Publishers
Attention: Sales Department
15 West 26th Street
New York, NY 10010
212/685-6610 FAX 212/685-1307

Visit our website:
http://www.metrobooks.com

DEDICATION

For my father, Roland S. Roberts

ACKNOWLEDGMENTS

Special thanks to my wife, Iris, for her critical eye, and to Ben Boyington

and Celeste Sollod for their editorial skills. Thanks also to Marge Kudrna,

John Lowrance and David Luther: *Sine bibliothecaris non scriptores*.

MEDITERRANEAN SEA

GAZA

SAIS
TANIS
ABUSIR
QANTARA
LakeTimsah
Bitter Lake

Wadi Natrum
HELIOPOLIS
GIZA
MAADI
ABUSIR
OMARI
SAQQARA
MEMPHIS
DAHSHUR
GERZA
ITJTAWY
CROCODILOPOLIS
MADUM
THE FAYUM
LAHUN
HERAKLEOPOLIS

SINAI

WADI MAGHARA

BENI HASAN

EL-AMARNA

ASYUT

BADARI

Dakhla Oasis

ABYDOS
NAQADA
DEIR EL-BAHRI
KARNAK
Kharga Oasis
LUXOR (THEBES)

KOM OMBO

RED SEA

ELEPHANTINE
FIRST CATARACT

EGYPT

Miles

0   50   100   150

ABU SIMBEL
WADI HALFA
SECOND CATARACT

CONTENTS

A TIMELINE OF ANCIENT EGYPT

Virtually all dates in ancient Egypt are approximate, and none of the following years should be accepted as absolute. All dates here and in the rest of the book are B.C. unless otherwise noted.

700,000 B.C. Date of earliest hominid evidence found in Egypt.

250,000-200,000 B.C. Earliest *homo sapiens* evolve in Africa (no evidence at this early date for Egypt).

100,000-30,000 B.C. Egypt is a lush and forested area. Earliest evidence of *homo sapiens* in Egypt.

40,000-30,000 B.C. Aterian culture

13,000 B.C. Archaeological remains at Tushka and Idfu in Upper Egypt show presumptive evidence of agriculture.

12,000 B.C. Qadan culture

5500-4500 B.C. Badarian and Merimdan cultures. Agriculture permanently established. Physical remains indicate these people were direct antecendents of the ancient Egyptians who built pyramids.

4500-3300 B.C. Naqada, Gerzeh, and Maadi Cultures. Direct evidence of burial practices and tomb construction techniques that will influence the First Dynasty.

3300-3100 B.C. The era of Scorpion, Narmer, Menes, and the origins of the Egyptian state.

3100-2770 B.C. The First Dynasty and the beginning of the Old Kingdom.

2770-2649 B.C. The Second Dynasty

2649-2134 B.C. The Age of the Pyramids and the Third and Fourth Dynasty periods. The Step Pyramid at Saqqara and the great pyramids at Giza built. Other pyramid complexes at Medum and Dahshur also built. Khafre builds the Sphinx.

2465-2323 B.C. Fifth Dynasty and the end of Old Kingdom pyramid building.

2323-2150 B.C. Sixth Dynasty. The last dynasty of the Old Kingdom.

2150-2134 B.C. Seventh and Eighth Dynasties

2134-2040 B.C. The First Intermediate Period. Ninth, Tenth, and Eleventh Dynasties build capitals at Herakleopolis and Thebes. These are contemporary dynasties ruling different parts of Egypt.

C. 2070 B.C. Akhthoes IV, one of the pharaohs at Herakleopolis, writes *Instructions for Prince Merikare*.

C. 2060 B.C. Mentuhotep II, a Theban ruler, conquers Herakleopolis and reunites Upper and Lower Egypt. His reign lasts from 2061-2010.

C. 2050 B.C. *A Dispute Between a Man and his Soul* is written by an anonymous author.

1991-1783 B.C. Twelfth Dynasty. The first pharaoh of this dynasty, Amenemhet I, begins the period Egyptologists call the Middle Kingdom. Middle Kingdom capital at Itjtawy is built.

C. 1970 B.C. *The Tale of Sinuhe* is written.

1929-1878 B.C. Amenemhet II and Senwosret II begin the great irrigation project in the Fayum.

C. 1895 B.C. Kahun, the village for the workers who built the pyramids at Kahun, is built.

C. 1860 B.C. Senwosret III begins to consolidate the power of the pharaoh and curb the independence of the nomarchs.

C. 1825 B.C. Kahun medical papyrus is written.

1783-1552 B.C. The Second Intermediate

Period. Weak dynasties, the Thirteenth through Sixteenth Dynasties rule.

ᶜ. 1640 B.C. Hyksos invaders arrive and establish Fifteenth and Sixteenth Dynasties in Lower Egypt.

1640-1550 B.C. The Seventeenth Dynasty rules Upper Egypt from its capital at Thebes.

ᶜ. 1560 B.C. Hostilities between the Hyksos pharaoh Apophis and the Theban pharaoh Sekenenre begin.

ᶜ. 1560-1525 B.C. Intermittent warfare between Hyksos and Theban pharaohs.

1550-1300 B.C. Eighteenth Dynasty reunites Egypt and begins the New Kingdom—Egypt's greatest period of conquest.

1525-1505 B.C. Amenhotep I rules a united Egypt. Begins practice of building the pharaoh's tomb underground at a hidden location.

1500-1492 B.C. The reign of Tuthmosis I begins the conquest of foreign lands as far north as Syria and the Euphrates River.

ᶜ. 1500 B.C. The Ebers Medical papyrus is written. Also approximate date of *The Taking of Joppa* and *The Tale of Two Brothers*.

The village of Deir el Medina is built to house workers building Karnak and tombs in the Valley of the Kings.

1473-1458 B.C. The famous female pharaoh Hatshepsut rules Egypt.

ᶜ. 1470 B.C. Hatshepsut's architect Senemut begins her funeral temple at Deir el Bahri.

1458-1425 B.C. Tuthmosis III sole pharaoh of Egypt. He expands Egyptian Empire in Syria and Nubia.

ᶜ. 1452 B.C. Tuthmosis III wins the Battle of Meggido.

1458-1353 B.C. Great period of building begun by Tuthmosis III and carried through to the reign of Amenhotep III. Impressive temple constructions throughout Egypt, but especially at Karnak and Luxor.

1353-1335 B.C. Reign of Amenhotep IV, the religious reformer who took the name Akhenaten

ᶜ. 1348 B.C. Akhenaten builds Akhetaten.

1330-1320 B.C. Reign of Tutankhamun.

1307-1290 B.C. Reign of Sethos I, who restored the Egyptian Empire and the centralized power of the pharaoh and began an impressive building campaign throughout Egypt.

1306-1070 B.C. The Nineteenth and Twentieth Dynasties. The last great period of Egyptian power.

ᶜ. 1300 B.C. Sethos I signs a peace treaty with King Muwatallis of the Hittites (1310-1282).

1290-1224 B.C. Reign of Rameses II. Rameses continues his father's building programs and maintains a strong foreign policy on all the borders of Egypt.

ᶜ. 1286 B.C. Battle of Kadesh in southern Syria.

ᶜ. 1269 B.C. Rameses begins building his great temple at Abu Simbel.

1194-1163 B.C. Reign of Rameses III, the last great pharaoh of the New Kingdom.

ᶜ. 1190 B.C. Rameses III defeats an attempted Sea People invasion of the Nile Delta.

1113-1085 B.C. Reign of Rameses XI, last great pharaoh of the Twentieth Dynasty. During his reign Egypt is virtually divided in two, with Rameses ruling Lower Egypt and the high priest Amenhotep assuming pharaonic powers at Thebes.

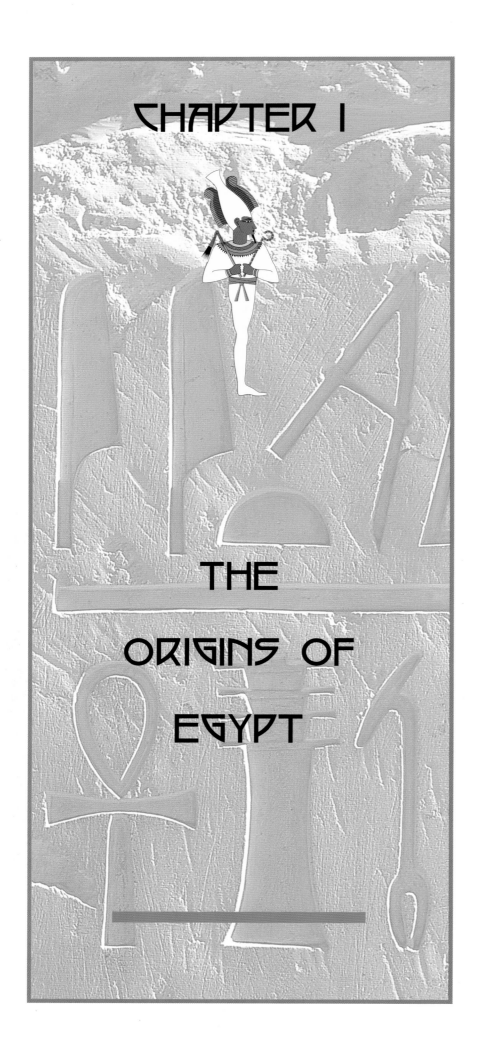

CHAPTER 1

THE

ORIGINS OF

EGYPT

GIFT OF THE NILE

The ancient Greek historian Herodotus traveled extensively in Egypt sometime around 450 B.C. and recorded a lot of nonsense about the country, but he was correct when he wrote, "Egypt is the gift of the Nile." Without that great river, Egypt would have been a desert wasteland whose contribution to world civilization probably would have been on a par with that of its modern-day next-door neighbor, Libya. Any consideration of the history of Egypt must start with an analysis of the power that the Nile has had over the whole of Egyptian civilization.

Egypt's climate includes some of the harshest desert conditions in the world. No place in the country receives more than 10 inches (25cm) of rain a year, and most of the country receives less than 1 inch (2.5cm) annually. From the Nile Valley east to the Red Sea, the eye sees nothing but rough, rugged hills interspersed with dry streambeds called wadis that fill with water only during brief, violent rainstorms in the winter months. To the west of the Nile Valley, the land sweeps toward the Libyan border flat and featureless—a giant, dry sea. Indeed, the western desert is so featureless that during World War II, the Allied and Axis armies that fought there used the stars, along with sextons and the techniques of sea navigation, to maneuver their large armies.

But running north through this barren landscape from the river island of Elephantine to the base of a giant delta spreading northward to the Mediterranean Sea is a narrow band of land paralleling both sides of the Nile that is brilliantly green with lush crops. This is Upper Egypt, one of the two regions into which the ancient Egyptians divided their country.

This narrow green aisle contrasts sharply with the bright red-and-yellow sand of the desert that spreads east and west to the horizon. In effect, Upper Egypt is a giant desert oasis, one that is 500 miles (800km) long but seldom more than 7 miles (11km) wide.

One hundred miles (160km) from the Mediterranean, the narrow river valley of the Nile separates into three branches that flow through a huge fan-shaped delta. Here the land along the riverbanks is low and marshy, with occasional high ground on which the ancient Egyptians built their villages

THE EARLIEST EGYPTIANS, 700,000-5500

By far the earliest signs of human activity in Egypt are found across the Nile from the famous temple complex of Rameses II, 150 miles (240km) below Elephantine. These remains, which date to about 700,000, are not bones but hand axes—large, roughly shaped, and generally triangular stone tools. All of them appear to have been crafted quickly with no regard for aesthetics, probably by smashing one rock against another until enough of one rock was knocked off to form a cutting edge. These crude axes were apparently the principal item in the ancient Egyptian tool kit for nearly 650,000 years. Because they are so prevalent at so many sites, many archaeologists believe that they were produced quickly and on the spot for a specific task and then discarded. No evidence exists to indicate that these axes were ever hafted to make a composite tool.

The early people who made and used these tools lived in an environment that was much wetter than the Egypt of the pharaohs (the classical and most familiar period of Egyptian history, from about 3100 to 31 B.C.). The Egypt of 700,000 or so years ago supported a climate and ecology that included lush forests where today there is desert wasteland. What is now the Nile River was a gigantic waterway a mile or more wide that flowed about five miles (8km) west of the current (and by comparison rather puny) Nile.

If we are disappointed by the crudity of these early axes, we can take comfort that they were not made by representatives of our species, *Homo sapiens*. Recent DNA studies of early human remains compared to earlier forms of hominids (the biological family

ly from which our species arose) indicate that *Homo sapiens* evolved only about 200,000 years ago. These early tool makers, therefore, were of a different hominid type than ourselves. Their remains clearly indicate that they were humanlike, so it is possible to make a few inferences about their habits, if we consider a few surviving artifacts. They must have hunted for food, killing their prey with rocks and sticks and then crudely butchering it with the ubiquitous hand axes. We can also assume that they lived in small groups because killing large animals with such limited tools required cooperative action. The fossilized remains of similar creatures found with hand axes in present-day Tanzania give evidence that hominid groups like these probably included about two dozen members dominated by six or seven males. The Tanzanian evidence includes stone circles that may indicate primitive huts or shelters. Beyond these few conclusions, it is impossible to say anything with absolute certainty.

Archaeologists must move forward in time more than 600,000 years before the traces of mankind in Egypt become clearer. At Dungul Oasis, Kharga Oasis, and Bir Sahara (all 50 to 200 miles [80 to 320km] west of the Nile), where water was once abundant, the human record is more apparent, and investigators have found evidence that the Egypt of 100,000 years ago was still lush and filled with wild game.

Circles of stones once again give presumptive evidence that use of the simple huts of earlier times continued in this era. While no human bones from this time have been found, vast collections of wild animal bones indicate that these people hunted

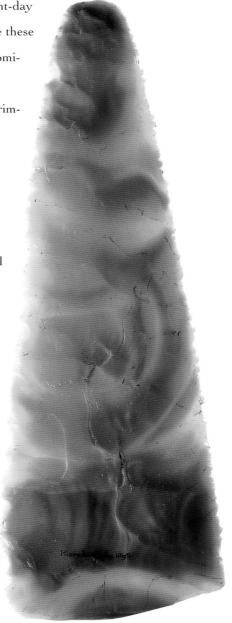

Below: A finely worked flint projectile is a stone descendant of the rough axes the earliest Egyptians used. Flint and obsidian were the basic tool-making materials before the Egyptians learned to smelt and work copper about 3400 B.C.

hippos, asses, gazelles, ostriches, jackals, and warthogs. It seems they may even have used ostrich eggshells as canteens—large numbers of these have been found in campsites. The Kalahari people in southern Africa still use these giant eggshells to carry water.

According to Michael A. Hoffman, the dean of Egyptian neolithic and paleolithic (stone age) studies, many tools of these early people are found in "fossil springs." Stone-age Egyptians lived and worked on the edges of oasis springs, and they seem to have periodically dropped things into their water supply. These artifacts became "cemented" to the sides and bottoms of the springs with minerals, and when a body of water dried up they were firmly fixed in place. In time, during the periods of a much drier desert climate, harsh desert winds eroded the land surrounding these ancient springs, allowing the former ponds, with their hard mineral outlines, to loom high and dry above the desert sands.

Using carbon dating, archaeologists can fairly confidently date many of these sites to between 100,000 and 30,000 or so years ago. All living things, plant or animal, contain a specific amount of the isotope carbon-14 in their systems. When an organism dies, its carbon-14 begins to decay at a constant, measurable rate into nitrogen-14 and carbon-12. Because this decay is both constant and measurable in a laboratory, no matter what organism it occurs in, scientists can estimate the amount of time that has elapsed since death.

However, there are problems with the process that an investigator must take into account. To begin with, after 100,000 years the amount of carbon-14 left in an organism is so small that it cannot realistically be measured. Secondly, samples can easily be contaminated by living organic matter that comes into contact with the dead sample. For instance, if a worm slithers into a decaying piece of wood and dies, then the worm's carbon-14 will remove years from the age of

the wood when it is evaluated via carbon dating, because the worm is younger than the wood. The only way to take possible contamination into account is to take numerous samples from an archaeological site, analyze them, and find an average date. If fourteen lumps of wood from the same ancient fire pit yield a date of around 14,000 and two yield dates of 7500 and 5000, then it is clear that the younger dates are the result of contamination.

There is another difficulty with carbon-14 dates: they are approximations that are often expressed in terms of plus or minus so many years. A carbon-14 date of 50,000 years may be off by 1,500 years or more, which to a layman seems a huge margin of error. Yet, for an archaeologist trying to establish a date for a site or a sequence of sites, it is a welcome fix on the past.

Using carbon-14 dating from a variety of sources, scientists have been able to date a sequence of prehistoric cultures that clearly evolve toward the classic and familiar Egyptian culture.

Aterian Culture

The first of these, the Aterian culture, flourished from 40,000 to 30,000 B.C. Even at so remote a date, this society evidences cultural antecedents of later Egyptian culture. The Aterian culture began during a period of heavy rainfall that allowed people to settle and to flourish far out into the area that is today deep desert. It ended with an extensive drought that slowly drove these people back to the Nile Valley and its dependable water supply. The Aterians were skilled hunters who pursued the same hippos, asses, gazelles, ostriches, jackals, and warthogs as did the people of 60,000 years before, but the Aterians did it with vastly more success because of an improved tool kit.

These people used microliths ("little stones"), tools that consisted of dozens of small, chipped flakes of flint, quartz, and obsidian cemented to wooden shafts with primitive glue (probably made from fish oil) to create comparatively long and extremely sharp tools. They also produced stone blades up to 9 inches (23cm) long that must have been attached to wooden shafts to make effective hunting spears. Some scientists believe that the Aterians may have used spear throwers, an intermediate stage in the slow transition from spears to bows. A spear thrower is a device that attaches to the back end of a spear shaft in such a way that when the spear leaves the hand, an extra thrust is added to the projectile. This construct adds range and striking force to a spear cast, but it is notoriously difficult to use, as modern archaeologists have learned by trying to use reconstructions. It was the kind of weapon that only a highly skilled hunter could have applied successfully.

By about the 13,000 B.C., the Aterian culture had evolved into more sophisticated societies living in large villages. By this time they were burying their dead in tombs that are vastly simpler forms of later Egyptian burial sites. Two of the cultures which evolved from Aterian cultures, whose remains investigators have found at Tushka and Idfu in Upper Egypt, may have even practiced an incipient and experimental form of agriculture perhaps as early as 12,000 years ago. The evidence of formal, deliberate agriculture is presumptive and open to question, but if further investigations support the contention, then we will find that ancient Egyptians were among the first to practice agriculture anywhere in the world.

The evidence consists of material remains that indicate a population concentration that would have needed a substantial and consistent amount of

agricultural produce for its support. The remains of microlithic blades polished to a high sheen indicate that they were constantly used to cut through grass and grain stalks that contain silica (particles of sand, usually of sand made from quartz specifically). In other words, these microlithic remnants probably once formed the blade of an early sickle. Further evidence comes from a large number of stone grinders found at these sites that must have been used to prepare cereal foods, and analysis of fossil pollens from the sites substantiates the presence of barley.

The Site 117 Graveyard

Forty miles (64km) southwest of Abu Simbel, on the east bank of the Nile, near the modern-day town of Jebel Sahaba, is a site that was part of this early experiment in agriculture. Known in the archaeological literature as Site 117, this spot was part of the Qadan culture, one of several that evolved from the Aterian culture. What makes Site 117 so important is that along with the remains of an ancient town there is also an extensive cemetery. Graveyards help archaeologists establish demographic and statistical information because they allow for so much comparison between individuals and grave contents that were interred roughly at the same time. For instance, differences in the quantity and quality of grave goods help determine class distinctions that existed in the society; differences in ages at death of those buried (apparent from skeletal variations) help determine average life spans for a particular group; and forensic analyses of human remains can help investigators determine what diseases plagued a particular group.

The fifty-nine burials at Site 117 reveal a great deal about life and death in the eleventh millennium.

The bodies were buried in shallow pits covered by sandstone slabs. They were interred in a flexed position with knees drawn up to the chest, the head of each individual turned to the left side, and both hands resting a few inches from the face. This form of burial may not have religious or ritual significance; it could simply have been the most efficient and labor-saving way to bury a human body in a time when digging tools were rudimentary. Generally, no grave goods were included with the bodies.

Forensic analysis has revealed that the bodies included twenty adult males, twenty-one adult females, eleven children, and seven bodies whose sex and age could not be determined. Many of the people showed evidence that they suffered from arthritis, various bone inflammations, tuberculosis, alveolar abscesses, and sacroiliac disorders, but also that none of them died from these ailments. By far the most common single cause of death was a wound caused by a stone projectile point that was still in the body at the time of burial. Twenty-four of the bodies—four children, nine males, and ten females, as well as one body of undetermined sex—held such stone points, and most points were found close to where a vital organ would have been in the living body.

It is certainly atypical to find that nearly forty-one percent of the "inhabitants" of a nonmilitary cemetery died by violent means. Frederick Wendorf, the excavator of Site 117's cemetery, offers the plausible explanation that these violent deaths were due to a period of strife resulting from the society's inability to practice its incipient agriculture (which in turn was probably a result of an increasing aridity in the area). Analysis of fossil pollens contemporary with this cemetery indicates a gradual drying out of Egypt at this time. One can speculate that most of these people died

as a result of raids on their village by neighboring groups who were competing for a gradually dwindling agricultural bounty. The fact that most of the homicide victims were women and children argues against death in formal battle, in which case most of the casualties would have been males of military age. It seems likely that the villagers beat back the attackers, for otherwise the dead would not have been given a formal burial. It is also probable that the victims died at roughly the same time, for most of the burials were multiple ones involving two or three people in a grave.

Site 117 gives a dramatic glimpse of an ancient society struggling with a real ecological crisis—a decline in rainfall. These people had no way of coping with this natural disaster. No evidence exists to indicate that anyone from this period had discovered how to turn the regular flooding of the Nile to an advantage.

It is not surprising, therefore, that after the eleventh millennium the grinding stones and the distinctive sickle blades with their characteristic sheen disappear from the archaeological deposits—at this time, these Egyptians probably returned to hunting and fishing. The descendants of the Qadan people at Tushka, Idfu, and Jebel Sahaba's Site 117 would have to reinvent or learn about agriculture from some outside source three thousand years later.

Opposite: The so-called MacGregor Man—named for the Scottish cleric William McGregor, who bought the 20-inch (51cm) object in 1922—supposedly came from Naqada, an early village and cemetery site near Thebes that was the center of intensive agriculture and trade as early as 5,500 B.C. Below: By the sixth millennium Egyptians had created advanced agricultural economies that allowed some people to specialize in producing art objects. This is a palette used to grind malachite to make green eye shadow.

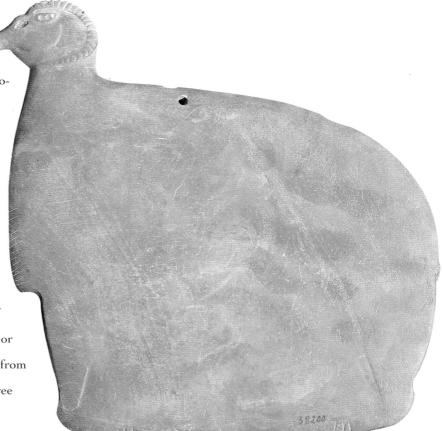

EGYPT AND AGRICULTURE, C. 5500-4500

Agriculture is the single most important invention of mankind during its long tenure on earth. Without it, humans remain wanderers subject to the movement of migrating animals. Agriculture makes possible the settled existence that we call civilization, which in turn allows for monumental art, literature, centralized political states, and scientific advancements. Ironically, civilization also seems to bring out the worst in man, for the accumulation of wealth in the hands of one people seems to result in the desire of other people to take it by sheer force.

Sometime before 5500, agriculture returned to Egypt. Its earlier discovery and utilization by the people at Site 117, near the town of Jebel Sahaba, had been an accident. The presence of agriculture in the early sixth millennium, however, was the result of a deliberate introduction of the process from the more advanced cultures to the east along the Euphrates and Tigris rivers—the area most people know as Mesopotamia, or the Land Between the Rivers. Archaeological excavations at Jarmo and Hassuna, near Mosul in modern northern Iraq, indicate that humans in the region began to farm as early as 8000. By around 5500, that technology had spread to Egypt. It does not seem that agriculture arose independently in Egypt because emmer wheat, one of the crops that the Egyptians cultivated in 5500, is native to Mesopotamia, not to Egypt. The whole transfer of agriculture to Egypt was facilitated by an increase in rainfall that had begun around 7000.

It is natural to assume that the Mediterranean Sea was the route by which farming traveled to Egypt because today it would be the most direct route between Mesopotamia and Egypt. But there is no reason to assume that this was the most direct route in the sixth millennium. It is more probable that this technology traveled to Egypt by a more roundabout route: first down the Euphrates or Tigris to the Persian Gulf, then around the Arabian Peninsula and up the Red Sea to the Wadi Hammamat, a long natural pass through the mountains from the coast to the Nile River Valley. From there, agriculture likely moved down the river toward the Nile Delta. There is no physically surviving evidence of a connection between Mesopotamia and Egypt at this early date, but by the mid-fourth millen-

nium there is plenty of evidence for this route in the form of pottery decorated with paintings of Mesopotamian ships that were found where the Wadi Hammamat opens onto the Nile Valley, just north of ancient Thebes.

Regardless of how cultivation techniques arrived in Egypt, their influence was dramatic. Suddenly, between 5500 and 4500, settled village sites whose economic base was clearly agricultural multiplied along the Nile and out into the desert where oases could support farming. Two of the more representative sites are found at el-Badari (c. 5000), about 50 miles (80km) north of Abydos on the Nile, and Merimda Beni Salama (c. 4800), 50 (80km) miles northwest of modern Cairo.

Badarian Culture

Archaeological and forensic analyses of the site at el-Badari clearly indicate that these people were the direct ancestors of the classical Egyptians. Their skeletal remains prove that they looked like the Egyptians of later ages, and their burials are obviously the antecedents of the much later and more elaborate classical Egyptian affairs. All Badarian burials contain funereal offerings, but some are much more elaborate than others. This has led investigators to assume that the contents of the tombs indicate class differences. Whereas most graves contain only a few pots and a simple necklace or bracelet, others contain numerous examples of distinctive Badarian black, brown, or red pottery that is polished and decorated with grooves, as well as jewelry made from turquoise, coral, and seashells clearly imported from the Sinai, the Red Sea coast, or even the far-off coast of Lebanon. Grave goods included as well clothing made of finely tanned

animal skins, woven mats, and stone palettes used to grind and prepare eye paint similar to that used throughout the rest of Egyptian history.

Also found here were small pots that contained castor oil and cosmetic cleansing oils. Perhaps these were used to treat eye ailments that were so common among later Egyptians—three thousand years later, Herodotus wrote that Egyptians suffered from eye diseases because of the blowing sand, but that they had doctors who were renowned throughout the Mediterranean for their ability to treat this kind of problem. Several of the richer tombs also contain female figurines with upraised arms and prominent breasts but no distinctive facial features; these are vaguely reminiscent of the famous "Venuses" found in many Middle Eastern neolithic sites. The more luxurious tombs also include finely chipped arrowheads, heavy stone maces, and throwing sticks that are duplicates of those pictured on New Kingdom tomb walls of the fifteenth century B.C.

Among all these spectacular tomb furnishings, the most exciting items are the small copper tools and jewelry that archaeologists have found in the richer ones. It seems that Badarian culture not only was the first to use agriculture (if we exclude the "accidental" discovery of the process at Tushka and Idfu), but it also marked the beginning of the use of metals in Egypt. All of the metal items found at el-Badari were hammered from naturally occurring copper—small copper awls, punches, drills,

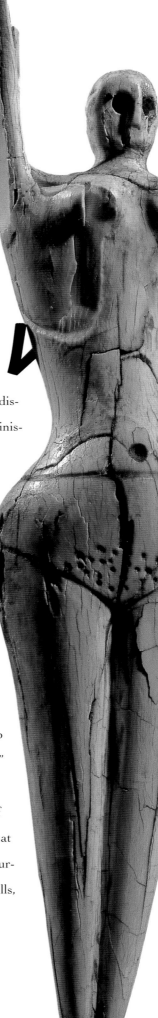

and pins. In this era, the Egyptians had still not developed the technology to smelt copper from ore and to use molds to form tools, but the Badarians apparently took the first step.

Merimdan Culture

The Badarians, however, were not the only Egyptians who were using agriculture and metals at this time. Farther down the Nile, in the great delta region, located just before the river flows into the Mediterranean, archaeologists have found the remains of another early agricultural group. They have named this culture Merimdan because its earliest remains were excavated at Merimda Beni Salama. Carbon dating of the site gave a date of 4800, plus or minus 420 years. Although this society clearly practiced agriculture successfully, their lifestyle was radically different from that of the Badarians. Similarities between the cultures exist in the form of stone palettes used for grinding cosmetics, and small copper tools. But the Merimdans practiced totally different forms of burial than did the Badarians and their skeletal remains indicate a distinct ethnic group.

The Nile delta was a place where high mounds were interspersed among low-lying marshy areas that were completely covered by the river's great annual floods. It was on these mounds, which stood out like islands during the annual inundation, that the Merimdans built their villages. As soon as the flood receded, they planted their crops, which they harvested in April and May, in time for the annual flood's replenishing of the soil.

Here, land that remained dry all year came at more of a premium than in the regions to the south, and while the Badarians could bury their dead on the edges of the desert, far from the floodwaters, the Merimdans interred their dead in graves within their villages. These corpses lay in shallow graves that were totally lacking in grave goods. This is unique in ancient Egypt, and has led to speculation. Hermann Junker, the initial discoverer and excavator of the site near Merimda Beni Salama, theorized that there were no grave goods because the families made offerings to the dead at their hearths within their dwellings. He noted that the dead were buried with their faces toward the nearest hut, a fact that seems to support his hypothesis.

The result is that with nothing in the tombs except bones, Egyptian archaeologists have for once found out more from studying how people lived than how they died. The Merimdans constructed their houses by first digging a hole about 15 inches (38cm) deep and 10 or more feet (3m) in diameter. They then surrounded the hole with walls about 4 feet (1.2m) high made of wickerwork spread with mud and straw. In the center of the house was a single timber that supported a conical roof which sloped down to the walls. Within the larger houses, there might be a wall dividing the interior in half, but all houses, regardless of size, had water-storage jars sunk in the floor and storage pits for grain, lined with woven mats, outside the home. The house site might include lean-to sheds and small huts for storage. Each house—along with its surrounding structures—was encircled by a 3- or 4-foot (1m) wall of wicker clearly dividing each homestead from the next. The entrance to a house might even

have a series of steps, made from the femurs of hippos, leading down into the interior.

Archaeologists at Merimda Beni Salama found a total of 125 bodies. The remains showed that the average adult male was 5 feet, 6 inches (168cm) tall and the average woman 5 feet, 2 inches (158cm) tall. Eighty percent of the 125 bodies at Merimda Beni Salama were women and children. The high proportion of female and child remains is consistent with similar cemeteries of ancient farming communities—infant mortality amounted to nearly 50 percent of all children born and women literally "bore" themselves to death having children, which are an asset in a farming community. In hunter-gatherer societies, where children are a burden because they mean more mouths to feed and because they can't hunt as early as they can farm, the number of child and female burials is usually not as proportionately large.

EGYPT ON THE EDGE OF CIVILIZATION, C. 4500-3200

With the introduction of agriculture, Egyptian culture became increasingly varied and complex, as is clear from the evidence at fifth- and fourth-millennium sites at Naqada, a few miles north of Thebes; Maadi, now a suburb south of Cairo; and Hierakonpolis, 75 miles (120km) farther south of Cairo. For the first time, evidence indicates towns that were almost large enough to be termed cities. We also find the beginnings of monumental architecture, sophisticated irrigation projects, and extensive evidence of foreign trade. By the end of this period, Egypt lacked only the unification under a single strong ruler that signified the beginning of the classic civilization of Egypt.

Above: In ancient Egypt it was necessary to build an elaborate system of canals, much like this modern one, to channel to the fields the water from catch basins filled after the flood. These irrigation systems were quite complicated and worked best when they were part of an extensive system, such as could only be achieved by a strong, centralized state.

Sir Flinders Petrie and Naqada

Sir Flinders Petrie, the "father of Egyptology," excavated a site called Naqada in the late nineteenth century A.D. Petrie pioneered meticulous scientific excavation techniques and recorded what he found in detailed notes. This not only allowed him to compare and contrast one site with another but also made it possible for later archaeologists to check and reinterpret his findings in light of later discoveries.

Such scientific exactness was new to the study of ancient Egypt. For at least a century before Petrie began digging, excavations had been dominated by men who can only be described as treasure hunters. People such as the notorious French art dealer Jacques de Morgan ransacked sites for large and spectacular pieces of art to sell in Paris. The worst of the lot, however, was Émile Amelineau, who not only shared de Morgan's lust for flashy, salable pieces but also smashed less spectacular examples of art to drive up the value of those he chose to keep. Fortunately for archaeology and for history, Petrie excavated with the utmost care and concern in order to maximize his understanding of the message of the place.

Petrie spent forty-two years digging in Egypt, but his greatest contribution to our knowledge of early Egypt was the work he did at Naqada. Between 1894 and 1895, Petrie excavated 2,149 graves in a seventeen-acre (6.8ha) area north of the ancient town. Most of the dead lay in rectangular pits roofed with a lattice work of poles, covered with brush, that was in turn piled over with a mound of earth. In time the pole roof collapsed, covering the contents of the graves with dirt. From an archaeologist's point of view, this collapse was fortunate because it brought the bodies into contact with the hot desert sands, which drew moisture out and preserved the bodies by a natural form of mummification. For the first time, ancient Egyptians were found with skin and portions of viscera intact. We have learned much more about the appearance of these people from these "natural" mummies than we have from simple skeletons. For instance, both men and women wore their hair braided and long, and the men were clean-shaven. The average height for men was 5 feet, 4 inches (163cm), and women averaged some 2 inches (5cm) shorter. By and large they looked just like modern Egyptians; in *Egypt Before the Pharaohs*, Hoffman remarks that these ancient Naqadans would escape notice among a group of modern Egyptians.

Grave offerings included finely chipped arrowheads, knives, and the occasional mace. There were also grinding palettes made of green slate, stones for mixing green and black eye shadow, and clay figures of ducks, falcons, chickens, and fish. But the most revolutionary findings, and the ones that show a clear link with the burial sites of later Egyptian society, were a number of large and elaborate tombs that clearly belonged to a higher stratum of society.

These tombs, set apart from the others, had been constructed with stone walls and floors. Each rich grave might hold as many as eighty pots, some decorated with black rims and red bodies, others featuring white geometric designs on a red background. Unique as the decorations were, the most surprising thing is that many pots found on the north wall of a tomb were filled with ashes, while pots found on the south wall held the remains of scented fat. Surprisingly, none of these vessels held any objects. Petrie conjectured that the pots on the north wall held the remains of personal property and firewood used to consume it in a ceremony before the burial. This may have been the beginning of the later practice of burying a pharaoh or noble with his valuable property. The deliberate destruction of the property before the burial might have served to awe the lesser people by illustrating the fact that the dead individual and his family had so much property they did not mind the destruction of some of it. The use of the perfumed fat in the pottery vessels on the south wall is unknown, but since the vessels appear only in the more elaborate tombs, it must in some way indicate class.

GERZEH

By 3500 this Naqadan culture had evolved into a more complex and materially rich one. Its later phase is often termed Gerzean, after a site in the great Fayum Oasis, west of the Nile, where evidence of the characteristics that define this culture was first excavated. Among this evidence was a new type of pottery made for the first time on a potter's wheel and decorated with red geometric designs, animals, or humans on a white base. Often the animals seem to be ibexes, water birds, or perhaps sheep, in association with people. But a fairly large number of these pots feature drawings of boats with crews in the act of rowing. Other examples show small houses drawn in association with an animal figure atop a pole.

These standards are the earliest representations of the totem animals of the nomes, the geographical divisions of ancient Egypt that later played an important part throughout Egyptian history. In later times, as we shall see, powerful political leaders created confederations of nomes and led them against other such confederations. Indeed it was the final subjugation of the nomes of Lower Egypt by those of Upper Egypt under the leadership of the semimythical kings

Scorpion and Narmer (c. 3100) that signaled the beginning of a united Egypt and its rise to greatness.

By 3300 the Gerzean tombs of the elite, found throughout Upper Egypt, had reached elaborate proportions. The interior walls are plastered and painted with pictures—a practice that became customary in later tombs. One of the most elaborate is found at Hierakonpolis. On this tomb's whitewashed interior walls are pictures of ships, some of Mesopotamian design. There are also depictions of hunters, two men engaged in a fight, and one man fighting lions. Another wall painting shows a man standing over a group of kneeling, bound captives, ready to bash in their skulls. This is reminiscent of the classic pose in which pharaohs are represented throughout

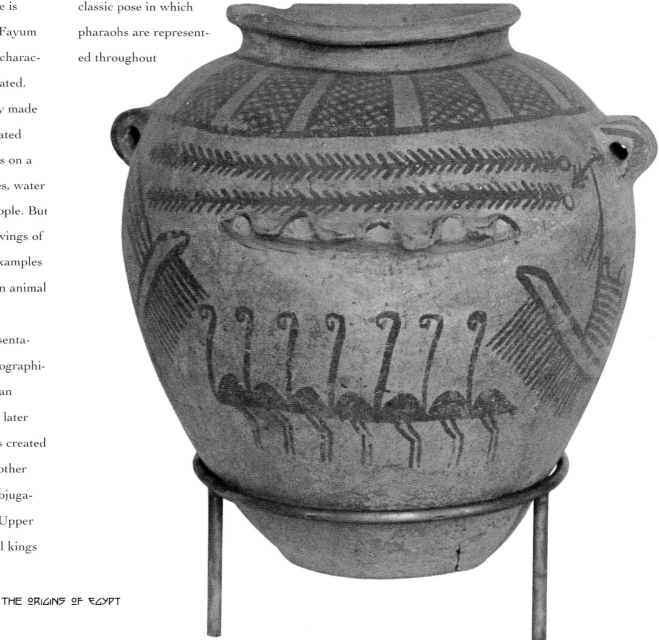

Below: A pot from the Naqada II, or late Gerzean, period, features characteristic red decorations on a buff background. The animals are probably flamingos.

Above: A detail of the Battlefield Palette, from the Gerzean Period, shows a lion, possibly a representation of an Egyptian king, devouring his enemies.

first discovered. It is distinct from that of the Gerzean cultures to the south. Instead of building elaborate tombs like the Gerzeans, these ancient Egyptians created a dynamic society built on foreign trade and the importation and manufacture of copper weapons and tools. Their excavated villages reveal houses that were built entirely underground and measured up to 24 feet (7.3m) in diameter. These "pit houses" not only served as living quarters but offered perhaps an extra measure of security for the often valuable contents.

Maadian artisans produced beautiful stone jars and palettes made from diorite, basalt, limestone, and alabaster. They also created jewelry out of carnelian and produced their own distinctive style of large storage jars, which were equipped with handles that would have made it easy to tie two of them together across the back of a donkey. In fact, excavations at Maadi reveal evidence of domesticated donkeys for the first time in Egyptian history. Finally, Maadi revealed evidence of copper works, where copper ingots were melted and formed into molds—the first true metallurgy in Egypt.

Even a casual survey of the remains of Maadi reveals that this culture traded with foreigners from the Sinai and Palestine. These foreigners perhaps brought across the desert copper ingots, carnelian, or cattle, which they traded for grain or manufactured items. Scattered throughout the Maadi site, sunken into the ground, are huge storage vessels that held bushels of barley or wheat. These specialized vessels could easily have been fitted across the back of a donkey as the perfect means of transport for nomads from the desert to carry away grain. Equally revealing of this trade with nomads are the earliest known remains of a corral that could have held the livestock that these nomads brought to town to trade. It is not too difficult

Egyptian history. The most famous of these scenes is on the stone palette (a plate on which royalty—both men and women—mixed their eyeshadow) of King Narmer, first king of the first dynasty of Egypt around 3070; another scene on the same palette depicts the king with a mace raised above his head, about to bring it down on the head of a defeated enemy. In fact this palette was excavated from the area immediately adjacent to an early temple at Hierakonpolis, a site where pharaohs throughout Egyptian history sent offerings to commemorate their ties with the founders of the Egyptian kingdom.

Maadi

Also in the Nile delta, contemporary with the sites at Gerzeh and the later tombs at Naqada, is a culture that archaeologists have named Maadian, after the site—Maadi—where artifacts which define that culture were to see these nomads as the ancestors of those ancient Jews who nearly two millennia later followed Abraham or brought Joseph into Egypt.

SCORPION, NARMER, AND THE ORIGINS OF THE EGYPTIAN STATE, C. 3300-3100

By roughly 3300 the Nile Valley supported well-organized societies of farmers who had come to grips with their harsh environment. These desert denizens, grouped in small villages along the banks of the Nile, had learned to cope with the annual floods of that great river by collecting the floodwaters in great ponds and releasing them gradually to nourish crops. They had entered the metal age by learning to mold copper into tools and weapons. They had perfected the arts of making pottery with the wheel, carving durable vessels from stone, and creating jewelry made from gold and semiprecious stones. They lacked nothing to advance to a truly great civilization—except unity.

These societies were divided into small local political units called nomes—twenty-two of them in Upper Egypt and twenty of them in Lower Egypt. Each nome had its own god or goddess and a local ruler called a nomarch. Although each nome had its own name, they are usually identified among Egyptologists by a number; for instance, the nome Hut-sekhem is known as the seventh Nome of Upper Egypt. In the century before 3100, however, a series of environmental changes, coupled with the dynamic leadership of two men, welded these tiny political states into a united and powerful civilization that would endure for the next three thousand years.

Since the 1940s A.D., scholars have pieced together an incredible story about the unification of Egypt under Scorpion and Narmer. We know practically nothing specific about either of them. It is possible that they were related, even father and son, and it seems that Narmer built on the political foundations that Scorpion had laid.

Archaeologists have found Narmer's tomb, and that of his wife Neith-hotep, but there is nothing in them to give a hint of the personality of either. Neith-hotep's tomb is at Saqqara, 80 miles (128km) from that of her husband at Abydos, and while some overly romantic and imaginative souls might want to infer that the distance signals some kind of estrangement, it is more likely that Neith-hotep, a princess of Lower Egypt, was buried in her homeland, while Narmer, a prince of Upper Egypt, was buried in his. There is an

Below: The famous Scorpion Macehead commemorates the unification of Upper Egypt into one cohesive state. The lion tail suspended from King Scorpion's waist is a symbol of royalty, and his crown is the traditional White Crown of Upper Egypt.

ancient legend that Narmer was eaten by a crocodile, and perhaps that is why there is no body in his tomb, but it is more likely that his remains were stolen centuries ago by that most enterprising group of professionals—the grave robbers.

As for Scorpion, some investigators infer that his name is not a proper name at all but rather a nickname designated to indicate the frightening and aggressive nature of this early ruler. While it is impossible to know anything for certain about Narmer or Scorpion, we can infer that both were smart, forceful, lucky, and probably brutal in order to be able to unite the small nomes, independent for centuries, into a single political entity in only their two lifetimes.

The discovery of various stone ceremonial artifacts reveals that the unification of Egypt began at Nekhan, on the west bank of the Nile about 30 miles (48km) south of Thebes. The Greek name for Nekhan was Hierakonpolis, or City of Horus, because it was the center of a cult to that god and the site of his temple. Horus, the special god of Upper Egypt, was the son of the Egyptian king and queen of the gods, Osiris and Isis. A renowned warrior, he killed his uncle Seth as retaliation for Seth's murder of Osiris. Horus' fierce nature was commemorated by his identification with the falcon, and in Egyptian mythology he is depicted as a man with the head of this raptor.

Throughout Egyptian history, all pharaohs sent offerings to the temple of Horus at Hierakonpolis. They were apparently copying a custom that had started long before recorded history began in Egypt, for the sands around the City of Horus have yielded thousands of artifacts that predate the age of the pharaohs. Two such artifacts that survive today offer clues which indicate that both Scorpion and Narmer used this city as their capital and began the process of unification from there.

The Macehead of Scorpion

The first is the Macehead of Scorpion. This famous object was found inside the temple of Horus at Hierakonpolis. It is an apple-shaped limestone macehead that measures 9 inches (23cm) high and is covered with carved reliefs arranged in three rows circling the macehead. When it was found, it was long smashed into dozens of pieces; when archaeologists reassembled it, they saw a scene that clearly represented a king in command of Upper Egypt overseeing the control of the annual Nile flood.

The middle row of the macehead shows King Scorpion with his *serekh* (a hieroglyphic representation of a person's name) clearly cut beside his head; holding a spade, he is dumping a load of earth into a basket held by a peasant. He is standing on the banks of a representation of the Nile that is surrounded by images of farmers and plants and forms the bottom row of the macehead. He is opening a dike wall to release water that has been stored since it was captured from the great annual flood of the Nile. We know this because he is set in a classic pose that appears in other, later representations of pharaohs we know are doing just that. Amenhotep III, a pharaoh of the Eighteenth Dynasty (1550–1307), appears to be doing the same thing in a relief at Karnak, the great temple complex near Thebes, dating from 1,800 years later.

Of itself, the sculpture of Scorpion would not be unique, since opening the dikes to irrigate the land was an annual symbolic act performed by all pharaohs throughout Egyptian history. This event demonstrated the power that the ancient Egyptians believed the pharaohs to have: the pharaoh was directly responsible for the coming of the flood. What is unique about the

representation on the Macehead of Scorpion is its symbology. The row above the ruler consists of a number of poles surmounted by representations of birds, mammals, and fish that are the individual symbols of the nomes of Upper Egypt. Suspended below each nome symbol by a rope is a bird, probably a sandpiper, the hieroglyphic symbol for an Egyptian. The message is clear: Scorpion has united all the nomes of Upper Egypt into one country, and as king of a united Upper Egypt he is officiating over the annual opening of the dikes to insure the continued well-being of his nation. Further evidence of his power over Upper Egypt can be seen by his portrayal wearing the White Crown of Upper Egypt.

Yet another representation of Scorpion's power are the remains of other nome signs on the other side of the macehead that have bows hanging from ropes. This is the traditional symbol of foreigners, in this case probably the inhabitants of Lower Egypt. While this does not illustrate that Scorpion had conquered Lower Egypt—otherwise he, like later pharaohs, would be wearing the crown of Lower Egypt—it does imply that he had conquered or at least attacked some of the northern nomes.

Left: The same White Crown of Upper Egypt that Scorpion wore on his Macehead is worn by Narmer on the famous Narmer Palette. The hieroglyphics on this palette are some of the earliest known.

The unification of all the nomes in Upper Egypt into one country was important because the ability to control the annual flooding on a large scale through the unified building of dikes and canals would give the region a tremendous economic advantage, implying concentrated wealth. Indeed, the very existence of the macehead at all implies a class of artisans, supported by the state, who had the time to create objects of high artistic quality that had no real use except to demonstrate the power of the king.

There is some evidence to support the idea that the unification did not grow solely out of Scorpion's design, but rather came about because of a gradual decline in the height of the annual Nile flood. The Palermo Stone, a large basalt stone dating to 2400, is covered with hieroglyphics that record specific events of the first five dynasties of Egypt (c. 3100–2323). Some of these inscriptions include the yearly level of the Nile. While there are no figures for the period before the era of Scorpion, the figures after 3100 clearly show a dramatic decline in the level of the flood. It is not, therefore, an unwarranted assumption that the flood had been declining in the years preceding 3100, the very years when Scorpion was in power. It seems possible, then, that this ruler used the lessened flood to mobilize the people around Hierakonpolis in an effort to conquer the Nile Valley and so maximize the effort to preserve and utilize what water there was.

THE NARMER PALETTE

The second item, the famous Narmer Palette, found at Hierakonpolis near the temple of Horus, clearly demonstrates that the unification of Egypt began in this city during the reign of King Narmer. The Narmer Palette is a 25-inch-high (63.5cm) slate slab inscribed on both sides with representations of Narmer, the first ruler to combine Upper Egypt with Lower Egypt, who may also have been called Menes. He is clearly identified on the palette by the hieroglyphic *serekh* that combined the sign for the word "catfish"—pronounced *n'r*—with the sign for "chisel"—pronounced *mr*. Together they form the sound *n'rmr*, which approximated the name Narmer.

On one side of the palette is the figure of the king wearing the White Crown of Upper Egypt and holding above his head a mace with which he is about to bash in the head of a defeated barbarian ruler dressed only in a penis sheath. There is nothing especially unique about this motif, frequently applied as a way of portraying a pharaoh dealing with a defeated enemy. But above the head of the foreign chieftain is the papyrus hieroglyph for Lower Egypt and, above that, in an obviously superior position, is the hieroglyph of the falcon, symbolizing Upper Egypt. To make the message of the palette absolutely clear, the falcon is holding in its claw a rope whose other end is attached to the papyrus hieroglyphic. Clearly, the palette is supposed to show that Narmer has defeated the ruler of Lower Egypt.

If there is any doubt about the front of the palette's message regarding the conquest of Lower Egypt, the other side, covered in four carvings, eliminates it. The topmost image repeats the *serekh* of Narmer, and the next depicts the king, wearing the Red Crown of Lower Egypt, surveying a battlefield strewn with headless corpses. A group of figures holding nome standards accompanies him. The third image shows two mythical animals with abnormally long necks that are intertwined in a circle—a perfect symbol for the unification of the two formerly separate areas of Upper and Lower Egypt.

Narmer may even have become powerful enough, with the combined wealth of the two Egypts behind him, to extend Egyptian conquests across the Sinai into Asia. Both sides of the palette depict western Asians in positions of subjection. On one side an Asian is trampled by a bull in front of the sign for a fortified city. On the other side are figures of two Asians in flight. Beside the head of one of them is the hieroglyphic symbol for Palestine—a bird's-eye view of a fortified city.

But it is not only the Narmer palette that preserves evidence of Narmer's power. When Herodotus wrote his *History* around 440, he included legends about the unification of Egypt. Herodotus had visited Egypt and collected information on the unification of Upper and Lower Egypt under Menes, which most (but not all) scholars believe was another name for Narmer. If these two were indeed the same man, then

Herodotus' account of the unification gives impressive evidence of the political genius of Narmer-Menes. Herodotus recounts that Menes, after uniting Upper and Lower Egypt, built a new capital city on neutral ground between the two regions. Herodotus further states that Menes demonstrated his power by building this new capital on land reclaimed from the Nile by the construction of a huge dike. In this graphic way, he demonstrated his power over the river that was the lifeblood of Egypt. The original name of the city was Memfer, which Herodotus and other Greeks corrupted into Memphis.

Narmer's unification marks the entrance of Egypt into history, not only because that unification made possible a prosperous economic base but also because his reign signaled the beginning of the use of hieroglyphic inscriptions. And it is with the advent of writing that formal history begins.

Above: On this side of the Narmer Palette, Narmer wears the Red Crown of Lower Egypt—a clear indication that he was the master of both parts of Egypt. His *serekh*, or hieroglyphic signature, composed of a picture of a catfish (pronounced *n'r*) and a chisel (pronounced *mr*) is clearly visible between the two bull heads.

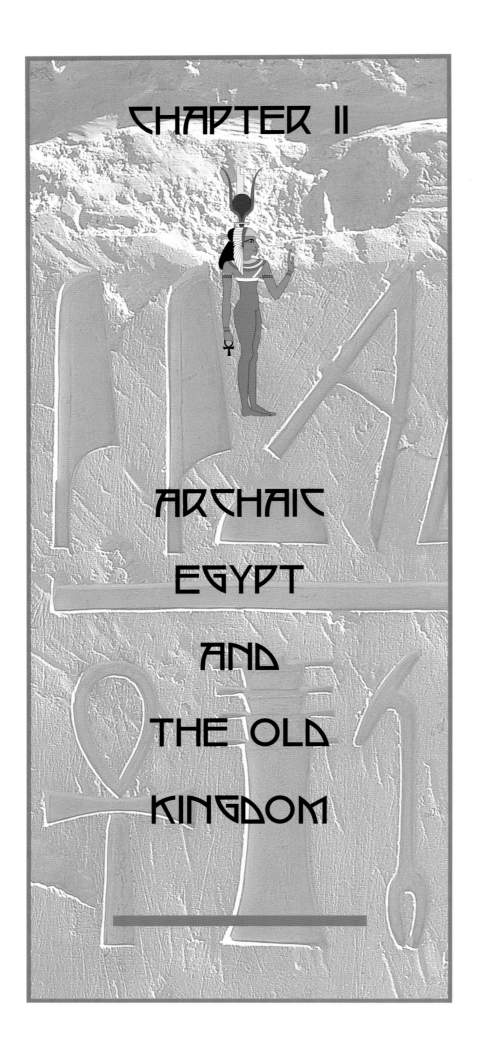

CHAPTER II

ARCHAIC

EGYPT

AND

THE OLD

KINGDOM

ARCHAIC EGYPT: THE FIRST TWO DYNASTIES, C. 3100-2686

For centuries historians of Egypt have used a chronological scheme of Egyptian history worked out around 270 by Manetho, a priest who lived in the Delta town of Sebennytus during the reign of Ptolemy II Philadelphus (r. 285–246; with kings, dates always refer to reigns; with other people, they refer to lifespan). By profession he was a priest in the city of Heliopolis but by avocation he was an historian, with access to the large library at Heliopolis, which contained records that went back to the earliest days of Egypt.

Manetho probably wrote history at the request of his new masters, whose dynastic founder, Ptolemy, had conquered Egypt with Alexander the Great and then stayed on to rule. In any event, he did what no one else had ever done—he wrote a complete history of Egypt, which he arranged by dynasties, or royal families, to give it a chronological orderliness. In the centuries that followed,

because subsequent discoveries of lists of pharaohs at Karnak, Abydos, and Saqqara proved the basic validity of Manetho's list, historians were willing to adopt his chronology of Egyptian history and hang their archaeological and historical studies upon it. Unfortunately, while we know the order in which events occurred throughout Egyptian history, we do not know their precise dates. All dates before 664 are approximations based on how different investigators interpret the astronomical events that the Egyptians "hung" their calendar on. Dates for early Egyptian history can vary from one Egyptologist to another by as much as eighty years.

The first division of Egyptian history, the Archaic or Early Dynastic Period, includes the pharaohs of the First (c. 3100–2770) and Second (2770–2686) Dynasties. During this period, Egypt became immensely wealthy as a result of the unification of Upper and Lower Egypt. The discovery and excavation of the tombs of the First Dynasty and Second Dynasty pharaohs at Abydos and Saqqara reflect the extent of this wealth.

Apparently, the transition from the First to the Second Dynasty was not peaceful. The First Dynasty tombs were ransacked and objects were stolen to be used in tombs of the Second Dynasty and to discredit the First Dynasty. Despite this theft, the richness of what was stolen reveals the archaic period as a time of tremendous economic growth. That richness also shows the tremendous emphasis these ancient Egyptians placed on life after death and how they planned to live in the afterlife.

The Egyptian view of death was rooted in the belief that the world was a static, unchanging place in life and in death. The position that one had occupied in life could continue unchanged after death if one made careful preparations while still living. A person's tomb (or simple grave, in the case of most people) needed to be furnished with items that would ensure a comfortable afterlife. It was best that these items be real, but if a person lacked the ability to furnish his or her tomb with actual items, then drawings, carvings, or other representations would do.

This belief apparently went as far back into Egyptian history and prehistory as it is possible for the investigator to go, although in the earliest periods of Egyptian history it seems that, for a short time, people believed life eternal was restricted to the pharaoh, his family, and those of his supporters and retainers whom he wanted to associate with in the afterlife. Gradually, however, as Egyptian culture matured, there was a democratization of death, so that by the period known as the Middle Kingdom (2040–1640) everyone who could make adequate preparations could aspire to eternal life.

Abydos

Archaeologists have found evidence of this belief in the tombs of the First and Second Dynasties at two Egyptian cities: Abydos and Saqqara. The former is located about 100 miles (160km) from the Mediterranean, where in ancient times the Nile began to divide into the seven channels that eventually formed the Delta. Here we see early evidence of the beliefs that later evolved into what motivated the building of the great pyramid complexes; the early

tombs here had burial chambers dug into the ground that held a rich collection of food, drink, weapons, clothing, and religious symbols. These goods were produced not only in Egypt proper but also were imported. Besides jewelry made from Nubian ivory and ebony, and lapis lazuli imported from Mesopotamia, these subterranean chambers were roofed with expensive, heavy cedar beams that had been imported by sea from Lebanon. The whole of the burial complex, whether it was a multi-roomed building or a group of buildings, was then covered with earth held in place by a rectangular retaining wall that measured about 7 feet (2m) high and was made of mud bricks. In its final form, the building resembled a large version of the *mastaba,* a rectangular flat-topped bench that stood in front of many Arab homes of the region.

The richness of these tombs was supposed to demonstrate the power and control that the early pharaohs had over the thousands of workers needed to maintain the great irrigation projects of the Nile Valley. In reality, the rich tombs only called attention to the vast wealth that they contained and which could enrich a brave excavator who dared to dig it up when the central government weakened or changed. In antiquity, tomb robbing was commonplace, and whatever escaped these ancient thieves was picked up by later ones.

One of the supreme tragedies of archaeology in Egypt was that the discoverer of the Abydos burials, Èmile Amelineau, was really nothing more than a

modern-day tomb robber. He was led to the place via stories told by the local Arabs, who called the place *Umm el-Qaab*, or Mother of Pots, because of the thousands of pieces of ancient pottery they contained. Amelineau was not disappointed, and between A.D. 1894 and 1898, he tore into the tombs without any attempt at systematic, scientific excavation and took away the best and most beautiful items to sell in his Parisian art shop. He also destroyed what he did not take away in order to drive up the prices of what he found, consigning thousands of pieces of pottery to oblivion.

This disgraceful behavior was partially redeemed by Sir Flinders Petrie, who excavated Abydos from A.D. 1898 to 1906. His carefully documented and orderly examination of the wreckage Amelineau left helped to place these tombs in their correct historical context. He found eleven tombs ranging from Narmer's (c. 3100) to Khasekhem's (c. 2666), and also excavated the hundreds of tombs that surrounded each of the pharaoh's tombs—the burial sites of nobles whose support of the pharaoh earned them a place with him in the afterlife. The pharaoh Djer, for instance, was surrounded by the tombs of 317 courtiers. Egyptologist George A. Reisner, writing in A.D. 1909, revealed that 162 out of those 317 contained the bodies of courtiers who were intention-

ally sacrificed so they could help their pharaoh to the next world. This practice, which anthropologists have termed *sati*, seems to have flourished during the First Dynasty, gradually growing in frequency until by the death of Pharaoh Den (c. 2820) nearly all accompanying burials showed evidence of *sati*.

At the beginning of the Second Dynasty (2770), this practice stopped. Anthropologists have noted that *sati* at the time of burial of a ruler is not an uncommon phenomenon at a certain stage of development in civilizations worldwide. However, the custom usually endures only for a short time, probably because succeeding rulers realized that by killing the most effective underlings of an earlier ruler they are wasting highly experienced and valuable assistants.

One "redeeming" factor in the sacrifices of the First Dynasty is that most of the victims appear to have been murdered before burial and, at least, were not buried alive. Far to the south in Nubia, an area that imitated Egyptian funerary practices, Reisner found gruesome evidence that hundreds of victims were placed alive in the tombs—the position of the skeletons clearly indicated that they died in an agony of suffocation.

Most of the sacrificed courtiers were buried in tombs separated from that of the pharaoh. The only exception seems to have been in the tomb of Djer, who flourished around 2890; here the pharaoh's wife, Merneith, was buried with him. Surprisingly, part of this noble lady's corpse survived both the ancient and modern tomb robbers—her arm, wearing four beautiful bracelets, was found stuffed into a hole in the tomb wall.

Excavations at Abydos also gave evidence of a steady advance in the prosperity of Egypt: between the beginning of the First Dynasty and the end of the Second, there is a noticeable increase in the size of the tombs. The first two pharaohs of the First Dynasty, Narmer and Aha, were buried in small tombs with a single storage room adjacent to the burial chamber; these rooms measured only 1,112 square feet (103m²) and 1,184 square feet (110m²), respectively. Tombs of the pharaohs Djet, Den, Semerkhet, Qaa, and Peribsen, dating from a later era, averaged 3,500 square feet (325m²), and the last king of the Second Dynasty, Khasekhem, lay in a tomb that was 10,784 feet square (1,002m²).

There is some evidence that the tombs, once they were built, were used as storage facilities for the pharaoh during his lifetime. These structures might also have served as clearing houses for tribute and taxes; when the pharaoh died, the accumulated goods often became part of his funereal trappings. Pharaoh Den's *mastaba* tomb apparently served this purpose, for it was built with a stone-lined ramp leading down into the chambers under the superstructure to facilitate movement of items in and out of the tomb. Qaa, a later pharaoh, had a tomb that contained forty separate storage rooms, each of which stored a different commodity.

Many of the items in these tombs were stored in beautifully carved stone jars made from extremely hard stone such as slate, alabaster, diorite, and crystal. The abundance of such labor-intensive items is a sign of the wealth of Egypt at this time, for only a rich society could afford to take laborers away from food production and set them to work producing items of a purely luxurious and nonutilitarian nature. The vast numbers of these jars—it was not uncommon to find the remains of a thousand or up to two thousand of them in a single tomb—also indicate that the Egyptian artisans had perfected a counterbalanced, flint-tipped drill that made for quick and efficient production of these funerary jars.

Saqqara

The tremendous wealth available to the pharaohs of the First and Second Dynasties is also apparent from the fact that at least six pharaohs and two of their queens were not content with one tomb each, but built two—one at Abydos and another 300 miles (480km) north at Saqqara. Measuring almost 5 miles (8km) long and a mile (1.6km) wide, Saqqara, a huge necropolis west of Memphis, contains tombs from all periods of Egyptian history. In the northern part, there are fifteen tombs from the First and Second Dynasties, along with accompanying tombs of nobles. Here, between A.D. 1929 and 1934, Walter Emery excavated not only hundreds of tombs of noblemen but also the tombs of the pharaohs Aha, Djer, Djet, Den, Anedjib, and Qaa, and he created one of the great controversies of Egyptology when he asserted that Saqqara, and not Abydos, was the true burial site of First Dynasty and Second Dynasty pharaohs.

The Saqqara tomb buildings were certainly royal in their decorations, contents, and size. In many instances, their exteriors were more impressively decorated than the exteriors of the tombs at Abydos. The outside walls of the *mastabas* at Saqqara had façades that included square pillars (reminiscent of the walls of palaces found on the contemporaneous Babylonian palaces), false doors and entryways, and were surrounded by brick curtain walls that enclosed entire tombs. Inside, numerous storage chambers were filled with luxury goods like those at Abydos, but the walls of the storage chambers at Saqqara were decorated with geometric designs, unlike the interior walls at Abydos, which were without decoration. The walls of the burial chambers were lined with wood and the rooms themselves were filled with furniture made of

cedar. In every instance, the luxury of the Saqqara tombs matched, and in some instances exceeded, that of Abydos.

The Real Tombs

So which group of tombs—Abydos or Saqqara—held the actual remains of the First and Second Dynasty pharaohs, and why were there two burial places for six of Egypt's earliest rulers? The answer is difficult and has inspired decades of scholarly debate. At present, most Egyptologists accept Abydos as the actual burial site, basing their opinion on the presence of Queen Merneith's arm in Djer's tomb at Abydos; despite the careful excavations at both Abydos and Saqqara, the queen's arm is the only evidence of a royal body from the Old Kingdom Period that has been discovered. All the royal corpses seem to have been removed in antiquity, either by tomb robbers or perhaps by order of succeeding rulers.

One question, however, remains: Why are there two tomb complexes? The first possible answer is that one set of tombs were cenotaphs, or fake tombs, built perhaps to confuse grave robbers. It is more likely, however, that the pharaohs built two tombs to advertise their power. In this early period, Narmer probably conquered Lower Egypt by force. Like many conquered peoples, the Egyptians of the Delta probably resented the control of Upper Egypt. We know from subsequent history that whenever the power of the pharaoh grew lax, the political connection between the two Egypts weakened and often broke until a strong ruler reunited them. The conquering pharaohs of Upper Egypt, therefore, built their real tombs at Abydos, near their homeland, but built equally impressive tombs in Lower Egypt to advertise their power and might.

Considered together, Abydos and Saqqara show that Archaic Egypt was an immensely impressive state that supported the ruling class in luxury. The contents of the tombs tell us that these early Egyptians engaged in trade with the more advanced civilizations of Mesopotamia. This latter region was the seedbed for Egyptian civilization, not only because agriculture came to Egypt from there millennia before, but also because, just before the unification of Upper and Lower Egypt, Mesopotamia had given Egypt writing, monumental architecture, and probably the theory of political unity under one leader.

Unfortunately, archaeology tells us nothing about the lives of the people who lived outside the royal world. No towns of the archaic period have been excavated and investigated. Furthermore, although these early Egyptians had writing, they used it only to record names and brief religious inscriptions. There was no literature in the form of letters, reports, or myths to reveal the inner workings of Egyptian society. We have to wait until the next period of Egyptian history, generally referred to as the Old Kingdom, to begin to get a more personal glimpse into the ordinary lives of these ancient people.

THE OLD KINGDOM: THE AGE OF PYRAMIDS, 2649-2134

Some time around the year 2686, change swept the last pharaoh of the Second Dynasty out of power and ushered in a new dynasty. This change could have been violent or peaceful; we do not have written records or other evidence to tell us what happened to bring it about. What we do know is that once the dust settled, Egypt had entered its most famous and picturesque era, the Age of the Great Pyramids.

It is difficult to comprehend the size of these great buildings even when standing next to one. Until the 512-foot (156m) spires of the Cologne Cathedral in Germany rose into the air during the thirteenth century A.D., the Pyramid of Khufu was the tallest structure

in the world. Even today, when the same cathedral is dwarfed by other buildings, the mass of the Great Pyramids still overwhelms the observer.

The Pyramid of Khufu is as tall as a forty-story office building, covers thirteen acres (5.2ha) (equal to seven city blocks), and contains two million stone blocks weighing in at an average of $2\frac{1}{2}$ tons (2270kg) each. This massive building was the result of architectural and religious forces that grew directly out of the traditions of the simple tombs of the First and Second Dynasties, which had themselves evolved out of the earlier tomb complexes at Naqada and Gerzeh. The architectural elements that made up these earlier burial sites were combined, adapted, and improved upon by one of the great geniuses of the ancient world, Imhotep, chancellor (or vizier) to the Third Dynasty pharaoh Djoser (2587–2564).

IMHOTEP

We know more about Imhotep than about any other commoner in the Old Kingdom. His father, Kanefer, was the chief advisor to Sanakht, the father of Djoser. According to legend, Imhotep was delivered via Caesarean section and rose through the administrative ranks because of his great intelligence. He is reputed to have been not only the pharaoh's chancellor but also a physician, architect, poet, and high priest of Amun. In the same tales, it is said that he habitually wore a leopard skin and was killed by lightning.

Long after his death, Imhotep was revered as a great healer and his tomb/temple was the site of pilgrimages by the sick, who brought embalmed ibises as offerings since that creature was his sacred animal. In A.D. 1935, the great Egyptologist Walter Emory excavated a temple of Imhotep at Saqqara hoping to find the great pharaoh's tomb. In a labyrinth of underground corridors, Emory found thousands of ibis mummies that blocked the passageways. Unfortunately, Emory died from a stroke while his project was still under way, and the excavations of Imhotep's temple have not been resumed.

We know tantalizingly little about the period of violence and civil war that preceded the rise of Imhotep's pharaoh, Djoser. Scanty evidence hints that Lower Egypt attempted to revolt against Upper Egypt around 2700, and for a time may have succeeded. It seems, however, that by about 2660 Pharaoh Khasekhem had, in a bloody campaign, defeated the rebels and reunited the kingdom; historians base this fact on a small statue that bears on its base an inscription stating that this leader had killed 47,209 of the "northern enemy." The enemy in question was undoubtedly the Delta Egyptians of Lower Egypt, and Khasekhem apparently made a significant impression, for there were no more revolts for more than five hundred years. Still, to cement relations, Khasekhem was careful to take a wife, Nemathap, from Lower Egypt. Through her, by an unknown series of events, the Third Dynasty (2649–2575) came to power after Khasekhem's death. It was during this dynasty that Imhotep made the contributions to Egyptian architecture and religion that were to endure for millennia.

Everything Imhotep did was predicated on preserving the power and prestige of the pharaoh. Because the pharaoh had come too close to losing control during the revolution that Khasekehm had quelled, a new religious emphasis and finer, more spectacular burial practices were instituted to convey the pharaoh's great power to the mass of Egyptians.

Sixty miles (96km) up the Nile from Memphis was situated the ancient temple complex of Heliopolis, which for centuries had been the center of an elite priesthood dedicated to the worship of the Sun God, Atum, in all his manifestations: Khepri, the morning sun; Re, the noonday sun; and Re-Herakhty, the sun for the entire day, from morning until evening. The polytheism of the Egyptians had always included Atum, but Imhotep made Atum the most important deity in Egypt, and made the pharaoh the god's personal representative on earth. Imhotep cast Amun as a god wearing the crowns of Upper and Lower Egypt who held the power of life, symbolized by the *ankh*, and the *was*, the symbol of political power.

Although the legend of Atum predated Imhotep and Djoser, it was during Djoser's reign that the creation myth of Atum began to gain popularity throughout Egypt—no doubt through the influence of Imhotep. In this legend the world was originally a featureless, water-filled void. Then a mound called a *ben-ben* arose from the water, and upon this mound was Atum. As Atum stood atop this *ben-ben* (the symbol of which was the pyramid), he

Opposite: The limestone casing visible at the top of Khafre's pyramid once covered the whole structure and was responsible for the smooth white appearance of these great tombs in ancient times. **Left:** On the north side of the Step Pyramid, this limestone statue of King Djoser sits in a small enclosure called a *serdab* and "looks" out through two holes onto a wide courtyard and a small altar. **Below:** A small, 7¼-inch-high (18.5cm) copper alloy figure shows Imhotep, the master builder of Djoser and the engineer who conceived the idea of the pyramid design.

masturbated, and from his semen came two lesser deities: Shu, god of the air, and Tefnut, goddess of life-giving water. These two gods produced children who became Geb, god of the earth, and Nut, goddess of the heavens. Geb and Nut had four children: Osiris, Isis, Seth, and Nephthys. These nine gods became the chief deities of Egypt.

By "advertising" that Pharaoh Djoser was the earthly manifestation of Atum, Imhotep made the pharaoh the supreme power throughout Egypt. It now remained to translate that theology of power into the physical symbology with which all Egyptians could see and experience such power. That symbol would be the illustrious Step Pyramid and its temple complex at Saqqara. Imhotep chose Saqqara not only because it was a traditional place of burial for the pharaohs of the First and Second Dynasties, but also because, like Memphis, it stood on the neutral ground between Lower and Upper Egypt; thus no Egyptian would feel alienated there.

The Step Pyramid

The Step Pyramid was a dramatic and sudden departure from any tomb that had preceded it. Originally, Djoser had intended to build a traditional *mastaba* tomb like that of the pharaohs of earlier dynasties, and in fact such a *mastaba* was built into the lowest level of the pyramid. The main tomb, dug into the stone underneath this *mastaba,* consisted of two chambers; the lower was the burial chamber, the higher a central treasure room with galleries extending out from it. The treasure room and galleries were decorated with blue tiles and stone-cut reliefs showing Djoser celebrating various religious ceremonies. When archaeologists excavated the burial chamber, it was empty except for

a single mummified foot. It seems these scientists had been preceded by tomb robbers.

Other subterranean rooms were also built into this *mastaba.* At the base of its western side, Imhotep constructed eleven subterranean chambers connected by shafts that went straight down for 108 feet (32.9m). These chambers probably held royal relatives. In one of them archaeologists found the mummy of a child—perhaps a son of Djoser. In another, excavators found the smashed remains of nearly 38,000 stone jars from the tombs of the First and Second Dynasties that had been carefully collected and stored here for safe keeping. Since their discovery, archaeologists have reassembled nearly eight thousand of the jars.

There is nothing unique about the design of the tomb of the Step Pyramid. What makes it important is that this *mastaba* was the first building anywhere in the world to be built entirely of stone. Earlier buildings had stone floors, lintels, or stelae in front of them, but the predominant building material had always been mud brick. With the completion of this *mastaba,* an architectural corner was turned.

Imhotep, it seems, was not satisfied, and he decided to change things even further. He expanded the dimensions of the *mastaba* on all sides to cover an area 360 by 410 feet (110x125m) and used the original *mastaba* as a platform upon which to build what seem to be three more *mastabas,* each slightly smaller than the one below. These distinct levels give the impression of steps—hence the name Step Pyramid.

Having finished this innovative building, Imhotep changed his mind, and added two more levels, bringing the structure to 197 feet (60m) in height. He then covered the whole of the outside surface with white Tura limestone, completing his modified design: a representation of the original *ben-ben* from which all

life had arisen under the benign hand of the god Atum. And since the pyramid was also the tomb of Djoser, the relationship between the pharaoh and the god who brought life was made abundantly clear.

The methods of construction for the Step Pyramid were just as original as its purpose. Although the structure seems to be just one *mastaba* stacked on top of another, Imhotep had in fact developed new architectural methods as well as a unique design. The internal core of the pyramid is made up of ten buttressed walls that slope inward against each other at a 75 degree angle. These walls gradually decrease in height as they get closer to the outside of the pyramid, and the decreasing heights of each wall account for the

pyramid's steplike appearance. Later engineers, realizing that this method distributes the weight of the pyramid evenly, would follow in Imhotep's footsteps. The only change to Imhotep's design would be to fill in the spaces between each step with stone to make the sides smooth from top to bottom and so achieve the classic pyramid shape.

Imhotep enclosed his dramatic construction in a stone wall measuring nearly 10 feet (3m) tall and a mile (1.6km) around. The outside of this wall was decorated with designs of paneled walls with vertical recesses, towers, and fourteen doorways, only one of which was real. Inside the walls was a mortuary temple, where the final funerary ceremonies took place

Above: Most of Djoser's temple complex at Saqqara has been restored over the last seventy-one years. This is a partial reconstruction of the mortuary chapel of Djoser within the enclosure of the Step Pyramid.

before the mummy was interred in the pyramid; a number of store houses for furniture and food; and a vast court that had two rows of small temples to the various nome gods of Upper and Lower Egypt. Also inside the wall was a royal "race course" around which a pharaoh was supposed to run at various times during his reign (the first time was always at his coronation, to dramatize his taking command of the kingdom).

On the south end of the enclosure stands an oblong tomb that was built for some unknown person. It has its own funerary temple and subterranean storage rooms. On one end of this temple is a large statue of a seated Djoser gazing into the temple through an aperture in the wall. Finally, there are a number of false buildings and temples; these structures have false doors and hinges and solid cores of stone, and many of them have stone walls that simulate reeds, papyrus

plants, and even palm trees. These stone houses represent crude huts such as might have existed in the earliest days of Egyptian settlement. Perhaps they represented the mythical houses of the first Egyptians that the God Atum created at the genesis of Egypt.

Hundreds or even thousands of laborers must have worked on this vast complex, but nowhere have archaeologists found traces of where they lived during its period of construction. Historians want to know more about the army of workers that lived here—what they ate, what they ate with, how healthy they were, what ailments they suffered from, what furnishings they had in their homes, and what aspirations they had for their own eternity—but there is no evidence.

The Fourth Dynasty

The ruins at Saqqara preserve only a glimpse of how a small, powerful elite lived. Unfortunately, this results in an incomplete picture of Egyptian society—one that would be similar to archaeologists in the future trying to reconstruct twentieth-century American life from an analysis of the ruins of William Randolph Hearst's 275,000-acre (110,000ha) estate at San Simeon, California. Fortunately, we have a more complete picture of Egyptian life during the succeeding Fourth Dynasty (2570–2460) and of the rest of the dynasties that make up the Old Kingdom (2575–2134).

Although writing was present in ancient Egypt long before the beginning of the Old Kingdom, the

Egyptians confined their literary efforts to recording titles, short epithets, and pious pronouncements on the stone walls of their monuments. Beginning with the Old Kingdom, however, Egyptologists have found more extensive works. Tomb inscriptions are much longer and more detailed. Actual papyri from the Old Kingdom have survived, such as those that Miroslav Verner found at Abusir in A.D. 1982. Other literary efforts have survived in the form of copies made by Egyptian scribes of the later Middle and New Kingdoms. Finally, legends about the great pharaohs of the Old Kingdom were passed down in written and spoken form until relatively recently.

That busybody Herodotus preserved the most colorful of these legends for us in the mid-fifth century B.C. During his travels throughout Egypt, he visited the temples, which held extensive libraries, and observed a priestly class that was happy to chide an upstart Greek about the glories of an older and wiser civilization — in much the same way that Englishmen of the late nineteenth century A.D. scorned upstart Americans. It is from Herodotus' chronicles that we learn about Cheops, perhaps the most famous pharaoh of all, whose Egyptian name was Khufu.

It was Khufu (2549–2530) who built the Great Pyramid, the largest of three pyramids from the Fourth Dynasty that dominate the landscape at Giza, northwest of Cairo. It is said that Khufu was obsessed with building this massive mortuary temple and that he spent twenty years of his reign completing the project. According to Herodotus, the project became a burden to the commoners who built it. When Khufu died, these workers and their descendants attempted to wipe out the unpleasant memories of their labor by refusing to call the structure Khufu's pyramid, instead referring to it as the Pyramid of Philition, after a local shepherd.

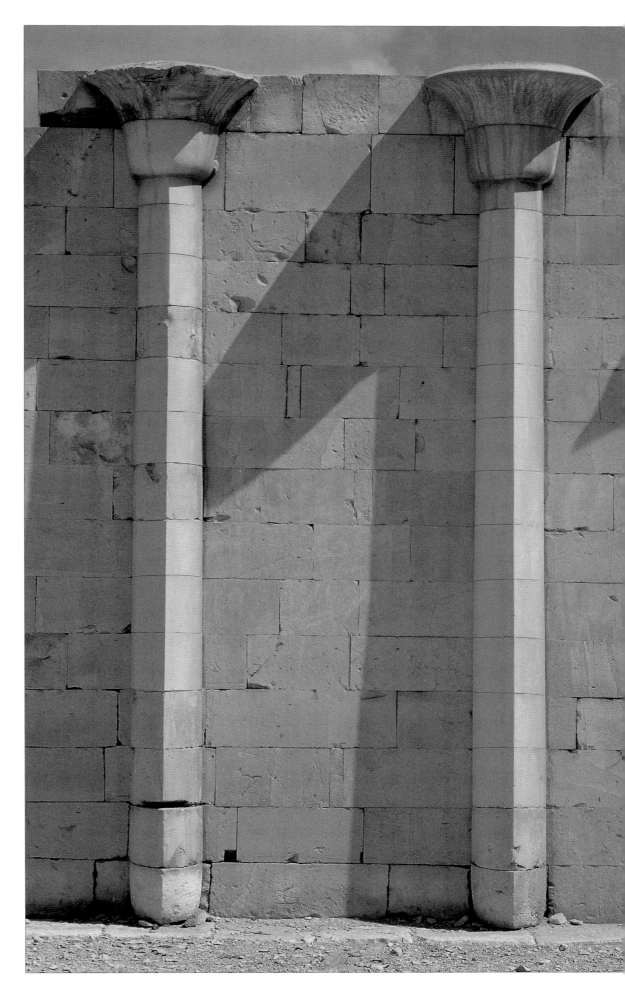

According to another of Herodotus' stories, when money ran short Khufu sent his daughter to work the streets of Memphis as a prostitute. This enterprising young woman, however, took the opportunity to levy a surcharge on her favors, with which she promptly constructed a smaller pyramid for herself. This story is certainly apocryphal, since Egypt did not begin to use money for another eight hundred years, but it does demonstrate the importance that pyramids assumed during the period of the Old Kingdom.

As can be seen from these tales, although pyramid building was common—and quite important—in ancient Egypt, it was not easy. Each of the pharaohs who succeeded Djoser during the Third Dynasty tried to build his own pyramid. Sekhemkhet, who immediately succeeded Djoser, also began building a pyramid at Saqqara, but it was constructed of materials that were much inferior to those used by Djoser. The next pharaoh, Khaba, began constructing a pyramid at Zawyet el Aryan, north of Saqqara; this structure was also unimpressive, compared to Djoser's, and it remained unfinished. These men ruled for a total of only eleven years, much too short a period of time to complete a really impressive pyramid. The last pharaoh of the Third Dynasty was Huni, whose reign lasted twenty-four years but whose pyramid at Medum, about 36 miles (58km) south of Saqqara, was not finished when he died in 2575.

The pharaohs of the Fourth Dynasty began a new era in construction. Their pyramids at Giza are the best-known pyramids in the world. Khufu's pyramid at that site was one of the Seven Wonders of the Ancient World, and it is the single largest tourist attraction in Egypt today. Building a pyramid is complicated, however, and at the beginning of the Fourth Dynasty, many technical problems had to be worked out.

Snefru

The first pharaoh of this dynasty was Snefru (2570–2551), whose experiments and disappointments in pyramid building are clearly preserved in monumental failures at Medum and Dahshur. Snefru apparently appropriated the step pyramid built at Medum by Huni early in his reign and started to convert it to a true pyramid with smooth sides. He originally planned a structure that would be larger and taller than Djoser's. The construction of the smooth sides, however, was imperfect and not firmly anchored to the inner pyramid core. As a result, the stones intended to smooth the sides slipped and fell into a huge pile of rubble around the base of the structure.

Undaunted, Snefru immediately started over. He apparently had ample funds—his armies had collected monies on successful campaigns into Sinai, where they captured the turquoise mines from the

Bedouin, and into Nubia, from which his troops reportedly brought back seven thousand slaves and 200,000 head of cattle. His second attempt was at Dahshur, about 6 miles (10km) south of Saqqara. The dimensions of this structure were truly impressive. It measured 620 feet (189m) on each side and 331 feet (101m) from top to bottom. The sides inclined upward toward the top at a very steep 54 degrees. However, when the pyramid's height had grown to 160 feet (50m), Snefru apparently became worried about the possibility of another collapse and decided to reduce the steepness of the angle to 43 degrees, resulting in a decidedly "bent" look.

While the Bent Pyramid, as this building is called, was sturdy with no hint of instability, its shape lacked a certain grandeur, and so Snefru decided to build still another pyramid, this one located one mile to the north. Called the Red Pyramid because of the color of its stones, this edifice was almost as large as the Great Pyramid at Giza. It measured 721 feet (220m) on each side and rose almost 325 feet (99m) into the air. Taking no chances this time, Snefru built the sides at a 43 degree angle. Snefru's is the first true pyramid in ancient Egypt.

Along with solving the structural problems of pyramids, Snefru's architects also showed their innovative abilities in designing the tomb chambers and the outside temple complexes that became standard features in later pyramids. All three of Snefru's constructions have burial chambers built into the structure of the pyramids instead of being excavated out of the rock beneath the building. Of course, this design led to new engineering problems—the pressure of the stones bearing down on these tiny open spaces could be immense, and collapse was again a frightening yet very real possibility.

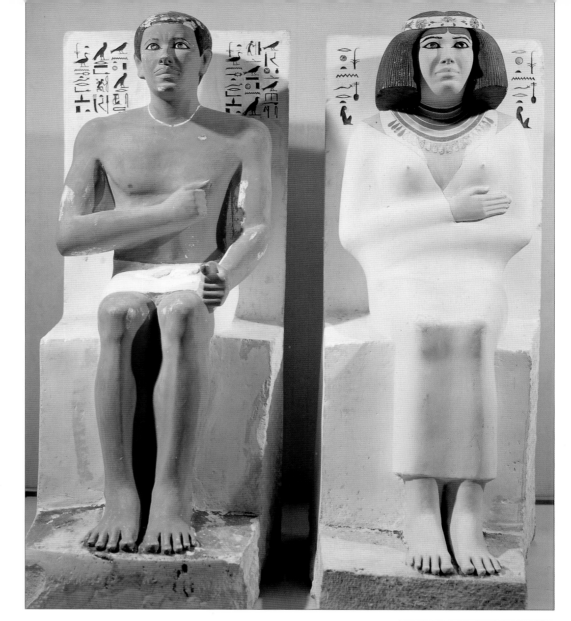

To prevent this problem, the architects built all three burial chambers with corbeled arches that directed the pressure down and around the chamber. Inside the burial chamber at Medum visitors can still see the ends of huge cedar balks projecting from the arches. Undoubtedly, these were among the cargo that Snefru had brought from Lebanon in forty ships, which according to records were 170 feet (52m) long.

At each of his pyramids Snefru built a temple complex. This innovation, which began with this pharaoh, was adopted by all subsequent pyramid builders. At the eastern base of each pyramid the architects built a mortuary temple to which the king's mummy was brought for special ceremonies at the time of burial. This temple was connected by a long stone

Above: A pair of painted limestone statues, remarkably preserved, show Rahotep, the high priest of Heliopolis, and his wife Nofret. Rahotep was the son of Snefru, the founder of the Fourth Dynasty, who ruled from 2570–2551.

causeway to a so-called valley temple that was near either the Nile or a canal connected to the Nile. After death, funeral officials floated the mummy down the Nile to this temple, where the process of embalming took place. The voyage down the Nile might have been a symbolic representation of the trip that the dead pharaoh's soul would take on its journey after burial to join the gods. Whatever its symbolism, the complex of temples and causeway became a standard architectural feature of the Old and Middle Kingdoms.

Khufu and the Great Pyramid

Snefru's son Khufu became pharaoh around 2551, and almost immediately began construction on his own pyramid. His Great Pyramid at Giza is the structure most people associate with Egypt—the pyramid which was to define the spirit of ancient Egypt. Even though pyramids were part of Egyptian culture for only a short period of time compared to the whole span of Egyptian history, they are what springs to mind when one hears the word Egypt. This is true not only for the modern world, but for the ancient world as well.

When the engineer Philon of Byzantium (flourished c. 200) identified the Seven Wonders of the Ancient World, he identified the Great Pyramid of Khufu as the most impressive of all. This pyramid, which is perfectly oriented to the four cardinal points of the compass, measured 755 feet (230m) on each side. It originally rose to a height of 481 feet (147m), but medieval Arabs stole the top 31 feet (9.5m), along with all of the white Tura limestone facing, to build bridges, walls, and mosques in nearby Cairo. The structure contained 2,300,000 stone blocks, each weighing an average of 2 1/2 tons (2270kg). To complete the pyramid within the twenty-three years of Khufu's reign, 274 of

these huge stones would have had to be set in place each day, a Herculean task even by modern standards. The pyramids were built by lots of men using simple but labor-intensive tools and methods.

More architectural wonders exist inside the Great Pyramid. The original tomb chamber, which measures about 28 by 46 feet (8.5×14m), was cut in the bedrock beneath the pyramid and was reached by a passage starting on the north face and descending 374 feet (114m) through masonry and bedrock. This chamber was never finished because Khufu, or his architect Hemon, decided to build another burial chamber 131 feet (40m) above the first, within the structure itself. This second room measures 20 by 16 feet (6×5m) and has a 20-foot ceiling. To reach it, a person has to ascend a 130-foot (39.5m) corridor that starts in the roof of the original passageway leading to the burial chamber in the bedrock.

But there is more; Khufu built a third burial chamber 32 feet (9.5m) above the second chamber that measures 34 by 17 feet (10×5m) and has a 19-foot (5.5m) ceiling. It is reached by a passageway about 154 feet (47m) long which is a continuation of the passage to the second burial chamber. This third passage is considerably wider and higher (10 feet [3m] wide and 29 feet [9m] high) than the first two, and for that reason it is called the Grand Gallery. One expects the Grand Gallery to be decorated with reliefs or paintings, but its only purpose besides offering access to the burial chamber was to hold giant granite blocks that could be released after burial to plug the lower passage to the Grand Gallery and the real burial chamber.

Both the third and second burial chambers have corbeled arches to support the weight of the pyramid stones above them, and the third and final chamber has five gabled arches of granite to further reduce

ARCHAIC EGYPT
AND THE OLD KINGDOM

Above: This stone relief from the tomb of the queen Meres Ankh, a wife of Khafre, was found inside her small pyramid at the foot of the pharaoh's at Giza.

♀ ⚱ ⚱ 𓏏 〰 ♀ ⚱ ⚱

strain from above. Two "air shafts" lead from the third burial chamber to the south and north faces of the pyramid. The northern passage is oriented exactly toward the north star. A giant sarcophagus of granite still sits in this third chamber, and not a single shred of evidence supports the idea that this giant tomb was ever used. Some people have suggested that it was a giant cenotaph, built to mislead the ever-present tomb robbers, and that the mummy of Khufu was secretly buried elsewhere.

Hetepheres' Tomb

Tomb robbers were a constant threat, even for a pharaoh as powerful as Khufu. In the midst of Khufu's reign, the mummy of his own mother, Hetepheres, had been stolen from her tomb, which was probably located near the Red Pyramid at Dahshur. Khufu had his mother's sarcophagus brought from Dahshur and reburied beside his own new creation at Giza in a small pyramid in front of his own. The mighty pharaoh would have been surprised and angered had he known at the time that his mother's body had been stolen, and that the sarcophagus he had so carefully moved was empty.

This fact only came to light in A.D. 1926, when George Reisner, an American archaeologist working for Harvard University and Boston's Museum of Fine Arts, discovered the entrance to the tomb where Khufu had buried his mother nearly 4,500 years before. Reisner was a painstakingly exact scientist who carefully documented every step during an excavation. When he discovered this entryway, sunk 99 feet (30m) into the bedrock on the west side of the Great Pyramid, he spent nearly a year recording and marking every artifact and its position as he dug down to the tomb chamber, even though he suspected almost from the first that he had found what no other Egyptologist had ever before found—a completely unplundered Old Kingdom royal tomb.

Before Reisner's discovery not a single royal mummy from the Old Kingdom had ever been found intact. They had all either been torn apart or taken away by robbers because they were covered with jewelry both on their limbs and within the linen wrappings around the corpse. Yet Reisner found no evidence that anyone had been in Khufu's tomb since it had been sealed. He even found remnants of food and drink offerings marked with the seal of Khufu that showed the pious son had made offerings to his mother after the burial. Reisner's careful work revealed the surprising fact that the tomb offerings in the burial chamber had been placed in the tomb in the reverse order that they were usually deposited. He was mystified when he found pieces of plaster in the tomb at Giza that fitted with broken pieces of the plaster lining around the door of Hetepheres' tomb at Dahshur 12 miles (19km) to the south. Nevertheless, when he reached the royal sarcophagus, he found the seals intact and fully expected to find Hetepheres waiting for him inside. He was surprised when he found that the giant box was empty.

In an amazing piece of detective work conducted some 4,500 years after the crime was committed, Reisner discovered a plausible explanation for the missing corpse. While Khufu was building his tomb at Giza, public attention had been diverted from the queen's burial place, enabling thieves to enter her pyramid and take the mummy. Alerted to the crime, Khufu had probably ordered the official in charge of Dahshur's funeral complex to investigate. The official found the body of the queen missing, realized that his life was in jeopardy, resealed the sarcophagus, and told the pharaoh that, although there had been a break-in, his mother's mummy was safe. Khufu ordered Hetepheres taken to Giza and reburied beside his pyramid in the small pyramid. He never suspected the duplicity.

Like all good detective work, this explanation covers all the facts. According to Reisner, the plaster bits in the Giza tomb fit with bits at Dahshur because the priests who gathered up the contents of the Dahshur tomb carried odd bits of plaster mixed in with the grave goods from one grave to the next. These same priests would also have removed grave goods from the Dahshur tomb starting from the entrance and deposited them in the inner part of the new tomb near-

est the sarcophagus—last in, first out, in other words. We can assume that the reburial was conducted with a certain amount of haste, to avoid public notice.

Reisner's conclusions even explain Khufu's bringing food offerings to an empty tomb: Khufu thought Hetepheres was still within. We do not know the name of the official who handled the cover-up, but it may have been Khufu's cousin Hemon, who not only built the great pyramid at Giza but also bore the title of Overseer of Works. A stone statue of Hemon survives from the *mastaba* tomb which Khufu allowed his cousin to build for himself west of Khufu's own pyramid. And in this representation, he does seem a bit smug.

The tomb furniture that was so secretly moved to Giza is immensely rich. There is a chest of silver bracelets covered with butterflies made of turquoise, carnelian, and lapis lazuli, all very small and delicate. Hetepheres was buried with her makeup kit, which included manicure tools, razors, and other beauty aids. Included in the tomb was a royal bed made from rare woods covered in gold and a delicate headrest also made of gold. Additionally, there was a chair of similar rare wood covered in gold. All of this furniture lay within a portable canopy made from gold-covered wood that at one time supported a linen sun shade. Everything was executed with exquisite taste, giving us an insight into the aesthetic sensibilities of this long-dead queen.

Above: The *mastaba* tomb of Ptah Shepses, the vizier of the Pharaoh Neuserre (2453–2422), is one of many at Abusir, southwest of Cairo, that contains four pyramids of the Fifth Dynasty. The tomb, whose roof is now missing, was one of the largest *mastabas* from the Old Kingdom.

Other Tombs at Giza

Khufu's pyramid does not stand alone at Giza. It is surrounded on the east, west, and south by row upon row of *mastaba* tombs of court officials and three small pyramids in a row along its east side built for Khufu's wives. The *mastaba* design predates the pyramid by a thousand years, but the *mastabas* at Giza were probably awarded to various officials for good and faithful service. These particular *mastabas* are simple in design. The burial chambers are sunk into the bedrock, and the stone *mastabas* are built over the tomb with shafts that run through the masonry into the rock below. After burial, these shafts were plugged up, and the families worshipped the deceased at special shrines built against the east sides of the structures.

In Khufu's day these shrines consisted of stone stelae that pictured the departed seated at a table piled high with food and drink. The walls and stelae of the *mastabas* were brightly painted so that rows of them gave a cheerful appearance and did not at all seem a dreary place. Indeed, ancient Egyptian religion painted a very real and precise picture of the afterlife, and people believed it to be an existence exactly like that enjoyed on earth. This happy state was not attained by everyone in the Old Kingdom; worthiness was determined only by the whim of the pharaoh. Once he had nominated a person for the afterlife by the gift of a *mastaba*, that person's participation in eternal life was safely assured.

Besides the pyramids for his wives, the *mastabas*, and the secret tomb of Hetepheres, Khufu's Great Pyramid complex revealed one more secret to excavators—large pits on the south and east sides. These pits contained real boats that had been broken apart and buried in airtight compartments. The boat excavated from Khufu's pyramid (three boat pits were empty, and a fifth boat pit has yet to be excavated) was 141 feet (43m) long, with a beam (the greatest width of the ship) of over 19 feet (5.5m), and a displacement of forty tons. It consisted of 1,200 pieces of wood and had six pairs of oars to guide it. For all its size, it was extremely unseaworthy and probably needed to be towed by other vessels. Its sole "practical" function was to carry the pharaoh's body to the valley temple of the Great Pyramid, where the corpse was ferried up the great causeway to the Pyramid Temple for embalming.

But the boats also served a mythological function after burial. Every morning, the dead pharaoh used the boats to accompany the Sun God Re across the sky, and every night he used another boat to sail across the night sky toward the dawn. The mythology of the solar boats was very old by the time Khufu built his pyramid, and it survived until the end of ancient Egypt, although the mythology surrounding their use changed over time.

Khafre's Pyramid

A few hundred yards to the west of the Great Pyramid is the pyramid of Khufu's son Khafre, who was pharaoh from 2520 to 2494. Khafre did not immediately succeed his father to the throne, for another son, Redjedef, ruled Egypt for eight years after Khufu's death. About 2530, Redjedef started to build a pyramid at Abu Ruwaysh, some 2 miles (3km) north of Giza, but construction was broken off at his death when the structure was relatively small, only about 39 feet (12m) high.

A pharaoh's pyramid remaining incomplete was rare, for a succeeding pharaoh of the same family almost always finished his predecessor's tomb (even though somewhat shoddily, in mud brick instead of stone). The fact that Khafre did not finish his older brother's tomb may imply some dark and unsavory family secret. One legend holds that Redjedef murdered his older brother, Kawab, to secure the throne, and that Khafre's decision not to finish Redjedef's tomb reflects his disapproval. Although there has been some initial excavation on Redjedef's incomplete pyramid, the burial chamber has not been discovered. It is possible that Redjedef was not buried in his pyramid, but at some other, less impressive site. Excavators did find some fragments of what had been excellent sculptures of Redjedef. These are the earliest examples of what were once free-standing, life-sized statues, a medium that would gradually become a hallmark of ancient Egyptian art. Ironically, the only statue of Khufu, who built the greatest pyramid of all, is a tiny ivory figure barely 7 inches (18cm) tall.

Khafre's pyramid is an impressive structure that is nearly as large as his father's. Before seventh-century A.D. when Arab builders stole the limestone mantles from all the pyramids at Giza, it measured 707 feet (216m) on a side and was 471 feet (144m) high, 10 feet (3m) shorter than Khufu's. However, the pyramid appears taller than Khufu's because it sits on a slightly higher piece of bedrock. Unlike Khufu's tomb, Khafre's pyramid is solid throughout. The burial chamber lies in the bedrock with a corbeled arch of granite covering it. Legend held that Khafre's pyramid had rooms and passageways within it just like his father's, and in A.D. 1970 Luis Alvarez of the University of California bombarded the pyramid with cosmic rays, a type of radiation, hoping to find voids within. This effort failed, however, leaving us to assume that the structure is just what is seems—a giant pile of limestone.

The Sphinx

Behind Khafre's pyramid are some tombs cut into bedrock that once contained his favorites; some poorly preserved *mastabas* on the east side of the pyramid appear to have been for other people who were associated with him. Yet the most renowned structure associated with Khafre's pyramid is the famous Sphinx that lies east of the pyramid. Along with the pyramids, the Sphinx is the most celebrated structure of ancient Egypt, and justly so, for it is unique among Egyptian antiquities.

This large statue measures 187 feet (57m) long and 67½ feet (20.5m) high at the head; it was carved out of a piece of limestone from which stone had already been taken to build pyramids. The builders also added stone to it to complete parts of the body and the paws that extend out in front. The shape of the Sphinx is that of a crouching lion with the head of a man sporting a *nemes*, the distinctive headdress worn by pharaohs. The *nemes* covers the top of the head and has flaps that hang down the sides, leaving the ears exposed; the ends of the flaps lie against the chest. This headdress bears a representation of a cobra's head—the traditional sign of Egyptian royalty—in the center. At one time there was on the face of the Sphinx a long goatee with a curled end, also a distinctive insignia of the pharaohs, but Turkish artillerymen destroyed the beard and the nose of the Sphinx by shooting at it in the seventeenth century A.D.

Originally, the Sphinx was supposed to be a guardian spirit for the necropolis at Giza. Its face was carved in the likeness of Khafre to demonstrate the power of the pharaoh during whose reign it was probably constructed. The Egyptians, however, quickly forgot whose face it was, and by the Middle Kingdom they believed that the creature was a representation of Re-Herakhty, the god of the Sun during the day. The name Sphinx is not an Egyptian name at all, but the moniker given to the statue by the Roman historian Gaius Plinius Secundus (A.D. 23–79), who may have confused it with the mythological Greek creature that had the body of a lion and the head of a woman and was famous for asking difficult, even unanswerable questions of human passersby.

Menkaure's Pyramid

To the southwest lies the pyramid of Khafre's son Menkaure, who succeeded his father about 2494. This structure is much smaller than either Khafre's or Khufu's pyramid: it measures only 344 feet (105m) on a side and 241 feet (73.5m) in height. The first sixteen courses of stone at the base are made of pink granite, but many of these stones were never smoothed and polished because Menkaure died before his tomb was finished. It was completed with mud bricks by his son Shepseskaf, who ruled from 2472–2467. The burial chamber was cut into bedrock 32 feet (9.5m) below the first course of stone.

When Colonel Howard Vyse, one of the first Englishmen to pursue scientific investigations in Egypt, excavated this chamber in A.D. 1837, he found a basalt sarcophagus, a wooden coffin, and a badly decomposed mummy consisting mainly of vertebrae and rib, leg, and foot bones. At the time it was believed that the mummy was that of Menkaure because the coffin lid had his name written on it. Once carbon dating became available, however, the coffin and the mummy proved to be from the second century A.D. Someone had apparently borrowed this magnificent pyramid. The basalt sarcophagus bore designs on the outside that represented a

scatters seeds; the oxen pull a plow that turns the earth, folding the seeds into the ground. The same relief also pictures a flock of goats being driven along after the plow so that their droppings will enrich the newly planted grain.

A stone relief at the mortuary temple built into the base of the pharaoh Sahure's pyramid at Abusir (constructed about 2455) features the earliest representation of Egyptian seagoing vessels. The vessel cut into this relief could have sailed either to Lebanon for timber or across the Red Sea to Punt for rare spices and exotic animals. It has a mast that supports a single sail and a steering post that controls a rudder made up of three oars. To the modern eye, the ship is peculiar because it has no keel; instead, the bow and stern are circled by stout hawsers connected by a thick rope that arches up and above the deck. In effect, this rope is an external keel which gives the ship enough rigidity and strength to navigate the relatively tideless Mediterranean and Red Sea.

We know from a *mastaba* inscription of the Old Kingdom that such ships reached the Red Sea by sailing down the Nile to Memphis, where they were taken apart and carried nearly 60 miles (96km) to the western arm of the Red Sea and reassembled. On the return voyage this process was repeated in reverse. Apparently nobody considered digging a canal or maintaining a permanent fleet on the coast.

Glimpses of life among the aristocracy are also preserved through the sculpture made for the valley temples of the pharaohs. Archaeologists have found statues of pharaohs, their consorts, and favored gods that allow a more intimate picture of noble life than had been seen in excavations dating to earlier eras. One such place is the valley temple of Khafre, which lies east of Khafre's pyramid, close to the Nile and just

in front of the Sphinx. It was from this temple, with its walls of polished granite and floors of even more highly polished calcite, that archaeologists recovered two 5½-foot (1.7m) diorite statues of Khafre. On each sculpture, a falcon—the representation of Horus as the Sun God Re—perches on Khafre's back with wings spread around the sides of the pharaoh's head. In this way the sculptor managed to create a clear message in stone that the king was guided by the voice of his god.

Another fine example of Egyptian sculpture is from the Valley Temple of Menkaure. This life-size statue shows Menkaure with his sister-wife

Above: The interior of Fifth Dynasty Pharaoh Izezi's vizier Ptah-hotep's tomb at Saqqara is shown here. Not only did he leave posterity with the finest wall reliefs of the Old Kingdom, but he also left a series of precepts that a person should live by.

Right: A three-foot-high (1m) statue shows the Pharaoh Menkaure standing between the goddess Hathor and the goddess of the Seventh nome in Upper Egypt, Bat. **Below:** The falcon behind the pharaoh's head in this statue of Khafre (5.5 feet [1.68m] high) is the symbol of Horus and implies that the god guides the pharaoh's actions.

Khamerernebti II. The two stand side by side, with Menkaure's right leg extended forward and his arms held rigidly at his sides in a classic Egyptian pose. Khamerernebti stands beside him, not quite so rigidly posed, with her left arm reaching behind her brother's back and her left hand visible around his waist. Meanwhile, her right hand crosses her body to touch his biceps. It is altogether a tender, wifely pose. While brother-sister marriages strike us as repugnant, Egyptian society accepted them as necessary for the pharaonic class, which traced its line of decent through the female line. There was certainly no better way to guarantee a pharaoh's right to the throne by blood succession than by marrying a female of his own family.

Another statue from Menkaure's Valley Temple clearly expresses the relationship between the pharaoh and the deities that ruled his fate. This slate statue, which was originally buried in a stone-lined pit, depicts Menkaure standing between the goddess Hathor, wearing her traditional horned crown, and the goddess Bat, who ruled the Seventh nome of Upper Egypt, and it is identified by the nome's hieroglyphic name—Hut sekhem—above her head. The pharaoh, wearing the crowns of Upper and Lower Egypt, seems to stride forward while the goddesses extend their arms behind his back and grasp his biceps in their hands. This representation leaves no doubt in the mind of the viewer that these deities both favor Menkaure and want to guide his every action.

Monumental sculpture was a new medium of expression for Old Kingdom artists, and even though the style is rigid and posed it still reflects the spark of creativity. Egyptian artists continued to repeat this style down to the Christian era, but as they became more and more distanced from the Old Kingdom their sculpture lost much of its originality, and by the beginning of the Middle Kingdom period, about 2040, it had become static and lifeless.

LITERATURE IN THE OLD KINGDOM

Sculpture and monumental architecture were not the only original arts to develop during the Old Kingdom: the period saw the development of its own highly original literature, primarily in the creation of the famous Pyramid Texts.

THE PYRAMID TEXTS

The Pyramid Texts were probably the single most important piece of literature for a noble Egyptian of the Old Kingdom, and certainly that culture's greatest contribution to world literature. Some authorities argue that in the early days of the Old Kingdom eternal life was something reserved exclusively for the pharaoh because he was the incarnation of Atum on earth. This custom, if it was ever true, soon gave way to the belief that the pharaoh could share this gift with his intimates.

By the Fourth Dynasty a very large proportion of the nobility of Egypt felt assured that they would live forever in the hereafter, provided they had won the approval of the pharaoh and were well versed in the ceremonies and prayers that the departed soul needed to make the difficult journey to the realm of the gods. Sometime before the end of the Old Kingdom, the approval requirement was abandoned, and to attain eternal life it was necessary only that a person know the correct forms and prayers. *The Pyramid Texts* fulfilled this requirement. It also described in detail the route to heaven and the state of existence a soul would experience once it arrived there. The oldest reference to *The Pyramid Texts* comes from the reign of the

Pharaoh Den, the fifth king of the First Dynasty. Apparently, the ceremonies and rituals continued to evolve from that early date until, by the reign of Pepy II, about 2152, they reached their almost final form.

The Pyramid Texts carefully outline the spiritual process of the soul, or *ka,* from death until it joined with the immortals in the afterlife. When the body was first placed in the tomb, it was helpless until the prayers in the sacred book were intoned by the family of the departed and the priests who officiated at the funeral. These prayers endowed the physical body with the ability to become a spiritual body, or *sahu,* which could then combine with the *ka* and, by a complicated process, move on to live with the gods in what was called the "Great Dwelling" of the gods.

While the *ka* is in the tomb developing strength for its journey, it can eat and otherwise sustain itself from the representations painted on the burial chamber's walls. During this transition, the *ka's* welfare is further provided for by furniture and other

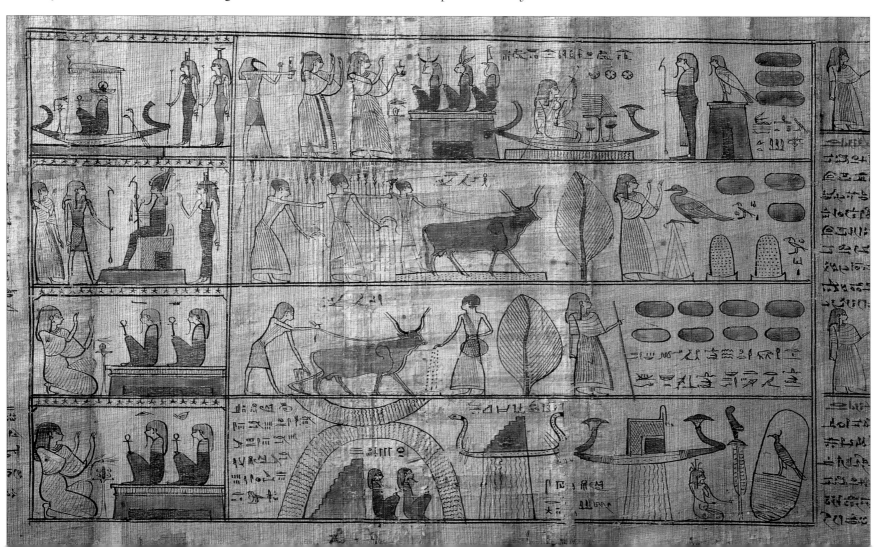

items the deceased used in life. Once the *ka* and the *sahu* are joined, they travel to the "Great Dwelling" as a *ba*. It is this *ba* that frequently travels through the sky on the solar boat accompanying the Sun God Re on his trips across the sky. Alternately, the *ba* lives in heaven in a variety of forms—perhaps as a shadow known as a khaibit or as a bright and shining image called *al khu*. Then again, the *ba* is liable to return to earth and the tomb to converse with the mummy. If the departed soul is that of the pharaoh, then it is ultimately united with Horus and becomes the Sun God himself.

Medical Texts

While *The Pyramid Texts* deal with mythology and the supernatural, other literary efforts from the Old Kingdom remind us that the ancient Egyptians had their practical side as well. It was during the Old Kingdom that Egyptian doctors began to systematize their profession by collecting descriptions of diseases and injuries and experimenting with treatments for these ailments. The physicians of the Old Kingdom took the first practical and scientific steps toward modern medicine. The earliest formal medical books date from this period.

The so-called Edwin Smith Papyrus was purchased from an antiquities dealer in A.D. 1862 by an American named Edwin Smith, who lived in Luxor, Egypt, between 1858 and 1876. The document was dated to about 1550, long after the Old Kingdom period, but grammar and vocabulary peculiarities indicate that the papyrus was a copy of a much older document. In twenty-two pages the unknown author deals with forty-eight different trauma cases using solid and logical methods of diagnosis that are similar to the processes doctors use today.

Like modern physicians, the ancient doctor first examined the patient's injury and questioned him about it. Then he made a formal diagnosis in which he decided whether or not he felt competent to deal with the problem. Finally, he clearly described the proposed treatment.

The Edwin Smith papyrus begins with injuries of the head and moves down the body to the waist. Unlike in later medical papyri, the emphasis is on realistic and scientific treatments. In only one case, where a part of the forehead had been smashed but the skin remained unbroken, does the physician resort to a magic incantation—he prays to the goddess Isis. Yet even here, his appeal is more in the form of a prayer that, except for the name of the deity, is little different from the prayer a modern physician might use after making all possible medical efforts.

Other treatments entirely avoid appeals to the supernatural and actually appear quite contemporary. Case number 35, for instance, is the description of treatment for a broken collar bone. After examining the patient and determining by palpation that the clavicle has been broken in two, the physician determines to treat the wound by placing the patient on his back with a wad of towels placed between the shoulder blades and then applying downward pressure on the shoulders until the ends of the clavicle come back together. Once that is done, the physician places a bandage on the inside of the upper arm and another against the side of the rib cage, then binds the upper arm to the body to hold the ends of the broken bone in place until they knit back together.

At times, however, this ancient medical writer finds an ailment he cannot cure. When this happens, he is honest about it. Case number 33 covers the problem of a crushed cervical vertebra. The examination reveals that one vertebra in the neck has been crushed and that the patient can neither talk nor move his arms or legs. A modern doctor would know that the spinal cord has been severed, but his ancient colleague, without knowing exactly why, realized that he was helpless to deal with the problem.

The one problem that plagued all ancient Egyptian doctors was infection. The physician who wrote the Edwin Smith papyrus accepted infection as a natural consequence of a wound that broke the skin. The normal treatment for such wounds was to cover them on the first day with fresh, raw meat, and on subsequent days with a layer of honey to prevent infection. The honey layer was usually covered with a layer of lint scraped from linen cloth, and the doctor changed the whole concoction every day.

John F. Nunn, a physician and world authority on ancient Egyptian medicine who is also an expert on hieroglyphics, has collected all the known references to ancient Egyptian doctors in a single volume. This collection and the accompanying analysis, titled *Ancient Egyptian Medicine*, lists the names of 150 physicians from throughout Egyptian history. Almost half of the physicians named from the Old Kingdom period have some royal connection. Many have a *mastaba* tomb near the pyramid of a pharaoh, or are mentioned in the tomb inscriptions of other royal supporters as having been granted the privilege of a tomb near the king. Most were called simply by the title "doctor," but some were identified by specialty. Inscriptions reveal that certain doctors dealt exclusively with internal medicine, proctology, ophthalmology, or dentistry. There may even have been special veterinarians. A number of animals—including hippopotamuses, crocodiles, ibexes, bulls, jackals, and cats—were sacred to the Egyptians, and it seems reasonable to conclude

that these important creatures would have been treated by doctors.

Evidence from the Old Kingdom suggests that medicine was not a profession restricted to men. Peseshet, a woman living during the Fifth or Sixth Dynasty, is depicted on the wall reliefs of her son, Akhet-hotep, as a physician. Peseshet is further identified as a supervisor of female physicians.

Numerous literary references from throughout the rest of Egyptian history name physicians who produced a wide array of medical texts during the Middle and New Kingdom periods. It is interesting, though, that later manuscripts are more likely to include magical treatments of disease and wounds instead of more scientific ones. Old Kingdom physicians appear to have been somewhat unique in their emphasis on the practical.

Above: Old Kingdom doctors used instruments like these bronze ones, but theirs were made of copper. Most of their medicine was crude by our standards, but it represented a serious attempt to study and treat diseases and wounds.

Behavior Manuals

The Old Kingdom was also a unique period of Egyptian history in other ways. At no other time in the history of Egypt was there a greater emphasis on order, stability, and correct behavior. For more than 250 years of its existence, there was no hint of rebellion, disorder, or discontent. Instead, the emphasis seemed to be on a society that accepted the pharaoh as its leader and everyone else occupying his or her natural position in life. Success was measured not in how ambitious one was but in how well that person performed the job he or she had been born into. Perhaps throughout the Old Kingdom, the emphasis on right action and correct behavior as anchors of society was a result of the orderliness and predictability of the rising and falling of the Nile. Just as food was plentiful if the Nile rose high enough every year, the people could expect to live successful and bountiful lives if they performed their duties as they were expected to.

It is not surprising, therefore, that many of the popular forms of literature in the Old Kingdom were books that detailed correct behavior. One of the most famous of these was *The Lessons of Ptah-hotep,* written by the chancellor to the pharaoh Izezi (2414–2375). In this book, supposedly written for the instruction of the royal heir at the request of the pharaoh, Ptah-hotep assures his audience that it will find success if only it follows certain precepts. The book begins with Ptah-hotep stating that he is about to retire from a long and happy life as the pharaoh's vizier. Ptah-hotep takes considerable space to complain about the ravages of old age: he has lost his short-term memory, standing and sitting are painful, his legs and arms hurt, he is deaf, nearly blind, and suffers from congestion. Still, amid all this misery, he has received a royal command to compose a book of instruction with which the pharaoh might instruct his son.

Ptah-hotep then lists thirty-seven actions that a moral person should do and believe to live the good life, not only because they are right in and of themselves but because by following right actions you are preparing the way for success. Among these directives are the following:

I. *It is possible to learn something from everyone no matter how humble they are. Even the lowest person can have ideas that may prove as valuable as turquoise, and it is ironic that a person can find good ideas in the conversa-tion of women doing the laundry.*

2. *If you hear an equal speaking well of a superior, agree with him. If an equal speaks badly of a superior, disagree with him. If an inferior speaks badly of a superior, ignore him, for such criticism is beneath you.*

8. *Faithfully carry out the orders of those above you.*

9. *Do not be jealous of the good fortune of friends, and do not out of spite remind others of their earlier shortcomings—it makes you look petty.*

11. *Take a break from work once in a while, but do not spend your vacation time working on the house.*

12. *Be sure to praise your children when they do well. If they are constantly evil and are a thorn to you, then throw them out of the house.*

13. *Be discreet in conversation and don't carry tales.*

14. *When an inferior asks you for something, listen patiently and kindly to him.*

15. *Do not be misled by a pretty face; women can make fools of men, especially old men.*

16. *Do not be covetous of friends' possessions. Lack of covetousness makes a man content with life and adds years to his life.*

17. *Be kind to your wife, because she can be your truest friend.*

18. *Be generous with gifts and praise to your servants and those under your command, because it will make them work harder.*

24. *When you sit in council with one above you, be silent, listen to the problem at hand, and speak only if you have a solution.*

26. *Do not approach your superior when you sense he is in a bad mood.*

29. *Never hold a grudge.*

30. *Trust not in wealth, for you can lose it.*

33. *Be careful in selecting your friends and choose those who do not gossip.*

37. *Do not let your mistress starve; it makes you look stingy.*

Autobiographies

The Old Kingdom has also preserved for us the first autobiographies. Through these documents, which were often written on the stone façades of nobles' *mastabas*, we gain the first glimpses of the real Egyptians, and they begin to become more than just names.

One such individual is Harkhuf, the governor of Elephantine, near the First Cataract. The walls of his tomb at this city contain information about his successful expedition to a place called Yam, which was probably somewhere south of the Third Cataract, in modern-day Sudan. He reflects pride through his boastful account of an overland expedition to Yam and his subsequent return along the Nile with a rich cargo of ebony logs, ivory, gold, and panther skins that he is sure will win him favor with the pharaoh. His most important cargo, however, at least in the mind of the eight-year-old Pharaoh Pepy II (2246–2152), was a black pygmy.

Harkhuf preserved on the wall of his tomb a letter from Pepy that the young pharaoh apparently sent up the Nile via a special messenger. The letter contains no acknowledgment of the other treasure that the governor brings with him, because the little pharaoh is most concerned that the pygmy reach him safely. The pharaoh, so the letter says, has heard about these small creatures—in fact, one of his predecessors had had one—and he wants Harkhuf to be especially careful. The pygmy must at all times be secured with a rope around a foot, so that if he falls overboard he can quickly be pulled back before he drowns. The pygmy is to sleep between trusted men, and someone must check on him ten times during the night. The boastful account of Harkhuf's expedition and Pepy's anxiety over the fate of the pygmy is the first real emotional image we have from ancient Egyptians, though such literature becomes more common later in Egyptian history.

The Common People

What about the common people? What does archaeology have to tell us about the people who built the pyramids and temples, and plowed the fields that created the wealth for the pharaohs? Surprisingly little, chiefly because their villages of mud brick either have not survived or have not been found. What has been found is a cemetery where these early common Egyptians buried their dead and a bakery where they made their food.

In A.D. 1993 Zahi Hawass, the director of the Giza and Saqqara pyramid complex, excavated a cemetery southeast of the Giza pyramids. In it he found the remains of six hundred people who lived at the time these pyramids were built. These skeletons showed the effects of the heavy work that pyramid building entails. Many had damaged vertebrae consistent with prolonged lifting of heavy loads. Still others were missing fingers, another consequence of moving stones that weighed tons up ramps. Yet amid all this, there was evidence that they may have had a certain pride in their work, for many of their small graves were decorated with mud models of the great pyramids.

In the same area another archaeologist, Mark Lehner, discovered an ancient bakery where these early pyramid builders baked their bread. The staple diet of the Old Kingdom Egyptians consisted of bread and beer. Egyptian bread was made with emmer wheat. The Egyptians did not add yeast to their dough; they did not yet know that yeast existed. Yeast simply collected naturally on the moist dough. The bread was baked in pairs of cone-shaped pots placed together to

Below: Although brewers generally used their feet to mash water-soaked bread to a pulp, this woman is using her hands to filter barley bread to make beer.

form mini-ovens. The bottom part of each "oven" was heated, along with the flour mixture, in a bed of coals, while the top half of the pot was heated empty. When both parts were hot enough, the top half was placed over the bottom and the "oven" was left to bake for an hour and a half.

Lehner did not find an Old Kingdom brewery, but he did uncover tomb reliefs and paintings that made it clear that beer was an important part of the diet. An ancient Egyptian would probably agree with the nineteenth century A.D. German proverb that states: "Beer is food." Egyptian beer was actually made from bread. When Egyptians baked bread, they set aside several loaves. They then placed the loaves in large jars of water and climbed into the jar and mashed the bread-water mixture to a pulp with their feet. In a few weeks, with luck, the pulp would fermented into a "beer" that was about 7 percent alcohol. The brew was then filtered through a strainer to remove the large chunks of bread that had not broken down. Even after straining, however, it was still very thick, and drinkers had to suck it up through a straw held with its bottom end near the jar's bottom to strain out what mash remained.

Perhaps someday archaeologists will find near the cemetery and the bakery the village of the people who built the pyramids, but this is unlikely since the modern suburbs of Cairo are already encroaching on the pyramid site at Giza.

THE END OF THE OLD KINGDOM

In 2152 Pepy II died, after a reign of ninety-four years—the longest of any monarch in recorded history. His death signaled the breakup of the Old Kingdom. There were still pharaohs and dynasties, but they were weak. The second-century historian Manetho claims that there were seventy of them. Around this time, Egypt entered its "dark age," a period Egyptologists have named the First Intermediate Period, which lasted for ninety-four years.

Although it seemed sudden, the collapse of the Old Kingdom had been seemingly inevitable for a century or more. It was aggravated by the gradually weakening rule of Pepy II, who may have been a powerful monarch in his youth, but in his dotage was unable to control the flow of events. The fault for the end of this culture does not lie just with Pepy, however. Long before him, during the Fifth Dynasty (2465–2323), things had begun to change. The first sign of weakness was that the pharaohs of this dynasty stopped building pyramids. The expense was just too great, and they had to be content with smaller, less costly tombs. This cessation of pyramid building was probably an economic necessity brought on by a decline in rainfall in central Africa that resulted in lower annual flood levels for the Nile, and consequently lower crop yields.

In certain years, the flood levels must have been extremely low, for according to one source it was possible to walk across the Nile. In times like these, many of the irrigation basins designed to hold the floodwaters during normal seasons could not be filled, and as a result the amount of productive land receded. This meant that although Egypt might still feed herself, only a drastic increase in the amount of work could bring about the same crop yields. This placed an increased burden on the common peasant, and signs of the commoners' resentment toward a nobility that still expected to live in leisure began to surface. In surviving sources from this period, there are accounts of riots in the streets and assaults on the homes of nobles that resulted in looting frenzies. Even some of the pyramids were broken into. In these same sources there are complaints that slave girls were wearing the lapis lazuli and carnelian jewelry of their former noble mistresses.

This kind of behavior certainly put a strain on the government, and the relatively simple administration that had surrounded the pharaoh had to face new, previously unimagined problems. To deal with these issues, the small central bureaucracy formerly made up exclusively of the pharaoh's relatives had to be expanded to include new men who were not related, and who were consequently not as trustworthy.

These men dealt with the social crises by brute force, and once they had reasserted control of the peasantry, they themselves became difficult to control. Many of them demanded more privileges from the pharaoh, including the right for their sons to succeed them when they died, so that during the Sixth Dynasty (2323–2150) these offices become hereditary, free from the control of the central government. During this same dynasty, these new nobles began to build their own palaces at the old provincial capitals of the nomes, instead of near the pharaoh's court at Memphis. These new leaders, called nomarchs, performed all the duties of a minor pharaoh: they ran the courts, organized the irrigation projects, and supervised the restoration of the canals and ponds damaged by the annual flood.

They also ran the local temples, and—most ominously—organized their own small bodies of troops. These armies were created to control the local rebellious peasantry, but later were used in raids against Egypt's neighbors. In time they were set against each other in civil wars.

The nomarchs amassed fortunes of such size that by the Sixth Dynasty they were beginning to build their own tombs, which were often as elaborate as the pharaoh's. For a time they were discreet enough to build their tombs away from the official burial sites near Memphis so that they did not appear to rival the tombs of the pharaoh, but by the reign of the pharaoh Teti (2323–2291), at the start of the Sixth Dynasty, the viziers Mereruka and Kagemni built *mastaba* tombs in the shadow of the royal tomb—and they were every bit as grandiose as the pharaoh's. This marked the beginning of the end.

By the end of the reign of Pepy II, at the close of the Sixth Dynasty, the nomarchs stopped even the pretense of respect for the office of pharaoh, and after Pepy's death they began to fight for the office among themselves. The great age of Egypt was history.

Above: The "famine relief" from the walls of the Pharaoh Unas' causeway at Saqqara shows emaciated Egyptians. Inadequate flooding of the Nile caused famine and helped to bring about the end of the Old Kingdom.

CHAPTER III

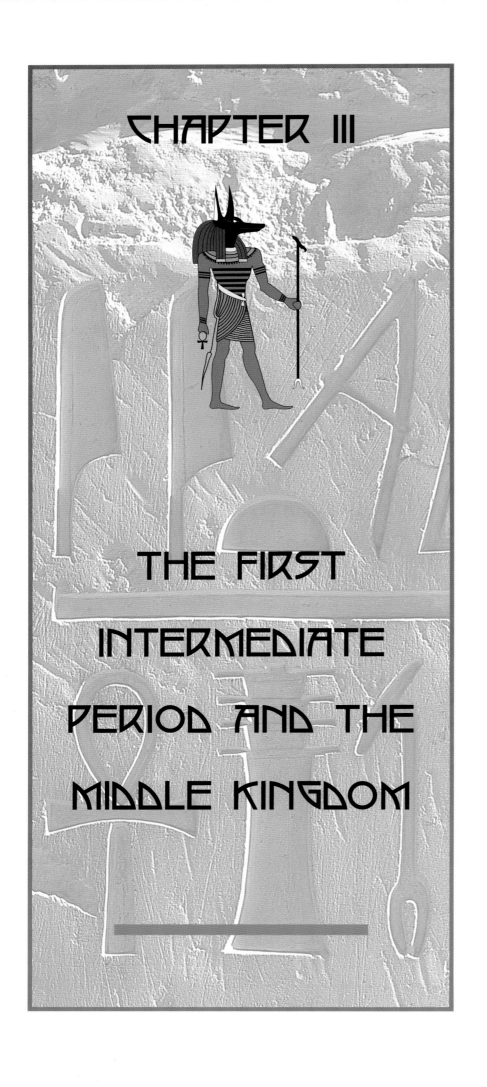

THE FIRST INTERMEDIATE PERIOD AND THE MIDDLE KINGDOM

Pages 66–67: The empty Old Kingdom tombs of Mekhu and Sabni, a father and son who ruled as royal governors in Aswan during the Sixth Dynasty, sit at the top of causeways the Nile used to reach. **Below:** Wood was a scarce commodity in Egypt, so most wooden furniture was small. This chest was made from sycamore and held together with pegs.

EGYPT'S FIRST INTERMEDIATE PERIOD, 2134•2040

At the end of the Sixth Dynasty, Egypt rapidly began to splinter into small geographical units that corresponded to the old prepharaonic nomes. This was more or less a normal way for the country to disintegrate in a time of crisis. Inevitably, during the Sixth Dynasty, as the central power of the pharaoh waned, the leader of each nome assumed more and more political, military, and economic power within his domain.

The Seventh and Eighth Dynasties (2150–2134) were periods of extreme chaos and disorder. The great tombs of the Old Kingdom were ransacked for their treasures and subjected to mindless vandalism which resulted in the destruction of countless statues and reliefs that could have revealed much about the early pharaohs and their world. The extent of this vandalism seems to indicate a deep rage on the part of the common people, who must have felt that their rulers had somehow betrayed them. This material destruction was matched by political disintegration. The ancient historian Manetho reported

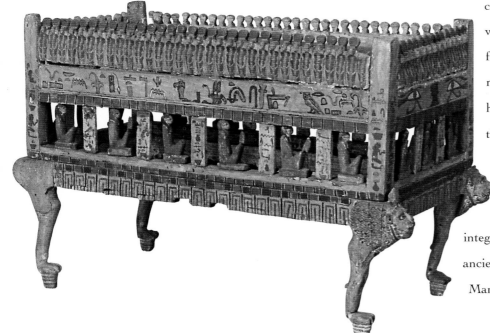

that at one point during this period there were seventy pharaohs in seventy days, with each assuming office only to be torn off the throne by angry mobs. While this may be an exaggeration, it probably does reflect the emotional turmoil of the common Egyptians, who were likely to replace a pharaoh who seemed to have no influence with the gods and could not control the annual rise and fall of the Nile.

All that remains of these weak rulers are their names, which were collected by later ancient Egyptians who wanted to record their ancient history. How long each reigned, and what he may have accomplished during his reign, remains unknown. Their pyramids and/or tombs have never been found. Perhaps none of these men ruled long enough to build anything significant. This possibility is supported by the fact that at the great stone quarries of Tura, Wadi Hammamat, and Hatnub, where most pharaohs throughout Egyptian history left proud messages chipped in stone detailing what they were going to build with their booty, there are no names at all of Seventh Dynasty or Eighth Dynasty rulers.

However many pharaohs there may have been in this chaotic time, the office itself had degenerated to the extent that the individual holding it was merely a figurehead; the real power was dispersed among the various and numerous nomarchs. Indeed, while archaeologists have not found names of pharaohs at the quarry sites of the period, they have found the names of powerful nomarchs who carried away stone to build their own mortuary temples and tombs, which were nonetheless only pale reflections of the earlier Old Kingdom funerary monuments. These regional leaders built their power locally, centered at an ancient nome, and "advertised" their successes on their mediocre *mastabas.*

At Dendera, capital of the sixth nome of Upper Egypt, just north of Luxor, the nomarch Mery bragged on a relief carved on his tomb stele that he had organized the harvest and protected the herds that fed the people. At Asyut, capital of the thirteenth nome of Upper Egypt, Mesehti, the local strongman, decorated his tomb with accounts of his campaigns against the Libyans and included model soldiers of forty Egyptian spear men and forty Nubian mercenaries that he used in his campaigns. These models are the earliest surviving representations of ancient Egyptian soldiers, and they make clear the primitive nature of warfare at this time. The soldiers went into battle barefoot and wearing only a kind of linen kilt around their middles. Except for the Nubians, who wore a thick leather pad on top of their heads, they did not wear armor. Their only weapons were copper-tipped, leaf-shaped spears, and rectangular, cowhide shields with pointed tops. No evidence exists to indicate that troops like these used any kind of tactical formation in battle. Organized warfare was in its infancy, and remained in a rudimentary state for six hundred years, until the advent of the New Kingdom.

Herakleopolis

Gradually, some degree of political unity in Lower Egypt was reasserted from Herakleopolis, a city south of the great oasis at Fayum that was sacred to the god Horus. Pharaohs of the Ninth and Tenth Dynasties (2134–2040) created a military and then a cultural center at this city.

At about the same time, 260 miles (416km) south of Herakleopolis at Thebes, a noble family had unified the nomes of Upper Egypt into the Eleventh Dynasty (2134–2040 — contemporary with the Ninth and Tenth Dynasties but in a different part of Egypt).

The greatest of the princes of Herakleopolis was a pharaoh named Akhthoes, whom Manetho identifies as a strong ruler, but one given to brutal slaughter and acts of terrible cruelty. However cruel he may have been, he was successful — so successful, in fact, that all of the subsequent six rulers at Herakleopolis chose to take his name. Akhthoes IV (c. 2070) is the only one of these men about whom any facts are known because he left advice for his son in a book called *The Instructions for Prince Merikare*. When this prince took the throne he became Akhthoes V; by this time political conditions in Lower Egypt had finally become stable, and the dictates in the book fit a political world where the rule of force is not the only way of a ruler. In many respects it is similar to the *Lessons of*

Ptah-hotep, which had been published during the Old Kingdom era. *The Instructions of Prince Merikare* instructs the pharaoh to be moral, patient, and kind to his people. It especially advises a pharaoh to study good speaking, explaining that a good ruler can win more battles by talking than by fighting.

The book also signals the beginning of a major change in the beliefs of the Egyptians of the Intermediate Period, a change that would continue into the Middle and New Kingdoms. In the last part of the book, Akhthoes IV discusses life after death, and it is clear from what he says that a profound theological shift has taken place. During the Old Kingdom, eternal bliss among the gods was the special possession of the pharaoh, his family, and his friends. In the midst of the chaotic twenty-second millennium, however, eternity seemed to become available to more people, particularly everyone who was pious and lived a life free of evil deeds. Such people, it was believed, would someday enjoy a special relationship with the gods. Akhthoes does not exclude evildoers from eternal life—he merely states that a person who does good deeds will earn a better place in eternity than one who does evil. By the end of the Intermediate Period, the theology of Egyptians had changed profoundly, and this new belief system continued to develop into the Middle Kingdom.

For a time the pharaohs at Herakleopolis enjoyed a period of security in Egypt's Delta. They not only brought order and peace out of social chaos, but also successfully defeated raiders from Palestine and built impressive fortresses to guard their frontier in the Sinai. They were even able to temporarily reopen trade with Lebanon. Some 280 miles (448km) to the south, however, a new power was growing based around the ancient village of Thebes, which was to become the capital of a united Egypt.

THEBES

The fortunes of Thebes were tied to a noble family that traced its line back to a woman named Ikui and her husband, Mentuhotep, who around 2250 had a son named Intef. This young man proved to be an especially forceful and aggressive noble in a world filled with such individuals. Like the descendants of Akhthoes to the north, Intef's successors chose to take their founder's name.

About 2134, Intef II took advantage of some political trouble in Herakleopolis to conquer the five southernmost nomes that owed allegiance to the Herakleopolitan pharaohs. Although Intef's advance was stopped in two battles on land and one at sea, he and his descendants held onto the five nomes. His son, Intef III, continued this aggressive behavior, adding a sixth nome to the budding empire. In 2060, a new Theban ruler named Mentuhotep II finally conquered the city of Herakleopolis itself, after a long and bloody war. (Mentuhotep I, his father, had been a local Theban ruler, not a pharaoh who ruled a united Egypt.)

The mass grave of sixty Theban soldiers that Mentuhotep buried with full military honors next to his own tomb site is dramatic testimony to this war. An especially skillful archaeologist, Henry E. Winlock, excavated the grave, and from the wounds of the soldiers concluded that they either had died in an assault on fortress walls or had, as they lay wounded on the field, had their heads bashed in with war clubs after the attack failed. Yet Winlock concluded that in the end Mentuhotep's troops must have won since it would otherwise have been impossible to give the dead a formal burial.

Mentuhotep ruled for over fifty years (2061–2010). He appointed either family members or close friends to every position of power in Egypt. With this, the power of Egypt—from the Mediterranean to the First Cataract—was uncontested for the first time since the Old Kingdom. In whirlwind campaigns the new pharaoh defeated the Libyans to the west, the Bedouins in the Sinai, and the Nubians to the south. For the first time since Pepy II's explorer Harkhuf brought back the pygmy (around 2238), Egyptian armies restored and guarded a trade route to Nubia. Mentuhotep also dispatched trading vessels to the Red Sea to trade with Punt.

When he died, Mentuhotep was able to advertise his power by being buried in a combination *mastaba* and temple at Deir el-Bahri, across the Nile from modern Thebes. Although today his burial site is completely overshadowed by the magnificent monument to the New Empire Queen Hatshepsut (who ruled Egypt from 1473 to 1458), which stands next to it, enough remains to convince us of his power and wealth.

This site was unique because it was the first tomb/temple complex to be built on different levels. The complex began with a now-lost valley temple that had a causeway at its western end leading up to large forecourt. The forecourt originally had gardens and groves of sycamore trees sacred to the goddess Hathor. Amidst the trees at the eastern end of the forecourt was a passage that had been cut into the rock and that led to a false tomb. On the western wall of this same forecourt reliefs depict Mentuhotep's conquests, expeditions, and other triumphs. These reliefs provide much knowledge about this pharaoh. The west end of the forecourt also has a ramp leading up to the next level, on which Mentuhotep's architects built a *mastaba* tomb. At one time colonnades and a roof allowed one to walk all the way around this *mastaba* in the shade.

The west wall of the *mastaba* level contains six mortuary chapels built in honor of two women who were undoubtedly the pharaoh's wives. Although his chief wife was his beloved sister, Neferu, at least two, possibly three, of these chapels belonged to wives who were Nubians. This was not the first time that an Egyptian pharaoh would seek his consorts from among the inhabitants of Nubia, for marriage alliances with a few of the rulers on that violent frontier would help guarantee the safety of Upper Egypt's southern border and would help ensure continued access to the gold, timber, and valuable skins of that region.

The entrance tunnel to Mentuhotep's tomb began in a courtyard directly behind the *mastaba* and led to a chamber dug 492 feet (150m) into solid rock. Another rock passage, designed to mislead tomb robbers, began in the courtyard in the front part of the temple and descended to a tunnel that led to a chamber directly under the *mastaba*. In the small room at the end of this passage was a statue of the pharaoh.

The ultimate compliment to the skill of Mentuhotep's builders is the great temple of Hatshepsut, a much larger imitation of Mentuhotep's complex that lies against this leader's burial site.

First Intermediate Theology

At the about the time Mentuhotep was cementing his power throughout Egypt, an unknown writer created one of the high points of Egyptian literature, a testimony to the disorders of the period and the misery endured by those who existed in it. In this long poem, "A Dispute between a Man and His Soul," the author considers whether suicide is a better option than continued life in a harsh and brutal world. In the first part, the narrator describes how he is reviled by everyone. Why this is so is never apparent, but the author's descriptions of how badly people regard him is graphic. His name, among his fellows, stinks like rotten fish, rancid meat, the muck from the bottom of a swamp, the droppings of birds, and the fresh dung of a crocodile.

In the second section, the speaker relates the mutual disgust of people for one another. The hand of each, he says, is raised against everyone else. The whole world lacks honesty, gentleness, respectability, morality, and compassion. A long series of verses describes how brother cheats brother, friends rob their friends during sickness, insolence pervades society, violence is everywhere, along with sin and sexual deviance. A man with a gentle disposition is the victim of everyone; an honest man must be cheated; and all lack the courage to look one another in the face.

In the third and final part, the speaker, disgusted with living, allows himself to revel in death. He compares dying to the wellness that follows a long illness, to the smell of perfume on a beautiful woman that is blown in one's direction by a kind wind which momentarily blocks the stink of the gutter, and to the peace a man finds when, after a long journey, he at last turns into the well-known path that leads to his home. Our speaker is convinced that in the world to come the decent man, who has tried his best to live a good life, will finally receive the reward for his efforts and live happily ever after.

Throughout the poem the modern reader constantly hopes for a moment when this ancient Egyptian might decide, as did the great Marcus Aurelius (r. A.D. 161–180) in his *Meditations*, that adversity builds character, and that it is, in a sense, good to suffer. But there is no such moment. It seems that, for the people of the First Intermediate

Period, suicide might have seemed a reasonable alternative to the utter misery of life.

The First Intermediate Period brought forth a theology to complement this view of death. The most profound change was that everyone could be welcomed into the afterlife. A new station in life would not, however, come with this eternal life—commoners would remain commoners and nobles would remain nobles in the great beyond. What had changed from the time of the Old Kingdom was the process by which one gains immortality.

During this period, numerous additions were made to *The Pyramid Texts,* and Egyptologists have found these preserved in the so-called Coffin Texts. These hieroglyphic passages, painted on the insides of wooden coffins that were cheaper substitutes for the stone sarcophagi of the Old Kingdom, detail the process by which the *ka,* or soul, must prove its innocence and become purified before it can be admitted to heaven. It was this detailing of the process that marks this period as one of religious innovation. The "proof" consisted of chanting magical phrases and performing certain rituals. In combination with a pure heart and exemplary life, these rites assured the supplicant soul of eternal life.

Of course, the journey of the *ka* was not easy—on the way to judgment, it would encounter demons, monsters, and strange phenomena that could cause its destruction. Only by reciting the charms written on the inside of the coffin could the *ka* avoid such

dangers as the crocodile demon waiting to snatch its food and supplies, forcing the *ka* to eat its own fecal matter to survive.

Even after a soul was admitted into eternity, it did not spend its time in blissful leisure. In eternity, the *ka* must perform work. For even nobles and pharaohs, in Intermediate Period and Middle Kingdom mythology, were required to perform manual labor in the fields of Yari, where the grain grew twelve feet (3.5m) high.

Yet the enterprising Egyptian had a solution for this. He or she would fill his or her tomb with innumerable figures called *ushebtis* (also known as *shawabti*), small human figures whose function it was to work long and hard in the great beyond in the place of its master. These figures were made from the wood of the *shawab* tree, and the well-stocked tombs of the First

Above: *Ushebtis* from the Middle Kingdom Period are the most common artifact found in Egyptian tombs, and literally thousands are for sale from art dealers throughout the world. Each one was meant to perform a specific task for the departed soul in the afterlife.

Above: These *ushebtis* are all from one tomb and are made of blue faience, or glazed pottery. **Opposite:** These gold and lapis lazuli statues are of Osiris, Isis, and their son Horus. The Osiris–Isis legends became popular during the Middle Kingdom. These statues are comparatively late, however, for they come from the tomb of Osorkon II (874–850 B.C.) at Tanis in the Nile Delta, but he could have stolen them from an earlier tomb.

Intermediate Period and all subsequent periods might have held hundreds of these figures, each for a different task. Since *ushebtis* were made of wood, and thus were not particularly valuable, many of them survived the inevitable rifling of the tombs by robbers. They are the single most frequent item found in tombs. Many tomb owners displayed the *ushebtis* working at specific tasks. Small models show dozens of *ushebtis* working together brewing beer, baking bread, and making wine. It is probable that the famous "toy soldiers" of the nomarch Mesehti were really *ushebtis* that the warlike official wanted with him to carry on his "work" of defending his nome in the hereafter. Archeologists have discovered that different styles of *ushebtis* are unique to particular dynasties. For instance, *ushebtis* made of dark stone are usually from the Middle Kingdom period, but *ushebtis* of wood that are crudely made are usually from the Seventeenth or Eighteenth Dynasties.

Isis and Osiris

It was during this same period that the legend of Isis and Osiris became popular and, to a large degree, became a rival theology to the cult of the sun god Re. According to this legend, at the time of creation, Osiris and his sister-wife, Isis, had given mankind the skills of civilization. They shared the world with Osiris' brother Seth and his wife Nephthys. The praise of mankind for the benefits Osiris had given them made Seth mad with jealousy, and he yearned to murder his brother. To this end, he built a magical chest that precisely conformed to the physical proportions of Osiris. At a banquet Seth offered a rich reward to anyone who could fit into the chest. Guest after guest tried and failed to meet this challenge. Finally, Osiris lay down in the box. Seth immediately slammed the lid shut, bolted it, covered it with melted lead, and threw it into the sea. He then assumed Osiris' place as chief benefactor to mankind, but his cruel and fickle nature made the world a terrible place to live.

Meanwhile, the chest floated to Lebanon, where it was washed ashore during a violent storm and came to rest in the branches of a tree. In time the tree grew around the box so completely that no one knew it was there. The tree was subsequently cut down by builders constructing the palace of the king of Byblos, and the section containing the box became a pillar in the throne room of this palace without anyone's realizing what was inside.

All the while, Isis had been faithfully searching for the box. She searched for years until she learned in a dream where it lay. She traveled to Byblos to persuade the queen there to intervene with the king and perhaps enable Isis to carry the pillar away. Her entreaties were successful, but when she returned to

Egypt with the box, the wicked Seth seized the body, cut it into fourteen pieces, and threw them into the air so that they became scattered all over Egypt.

The dutiful Isis set out again to find the pieces and reassemble them. She found all the pieces but for the penis, which had fallen into the Nile and been eaten by fishes. She managed to sew the body back together and whittle and attach an artificial penis, concluding by chanting magical words in order to bring Osiris back to life. Further magical chants enabled Osiris to impregnate Isis with his wooden penis. The fruit of this union was the god Horus. Soon after this miraculous resurrection and birth, Osiris left the earth to become lord of the afterlife, and Isis fled with the infant Horus to hide in the marshes of the Delta. There Horus grew into a powerful young god bent on revenge. As an adult, he returned and slew his wicked uncle Seth in a titanic struggle. He lost an eye in this contest, but assumed his rightful place as ruler of the earth.

This legend, of course, contains all the elements that guided the typical Egyptian in his or her quest for eternal life. Osiris had lived a good life, benefiting mankind in general. When he was killed by his brother, who represented evil, he was able to find resurrection through the magical restoration of his body, which led ultimately to his rule in heaven. So, too, a man or woman who lived a beneficial life on earth, and whose body was magically restored by the process of mummification, could ascend to heaven and be with Osiris. The fact that the legend became popular precisely during a period of violence, disorder, and evil is symbolic of the evil rule of Seth.

The Egyptians would continue to refine this mythology about death and Osiris, and its primary elements would come to dominate Egyptian history up to the Christian era. Despite its comparatively brief duration, the Intermediate Period must rank as one of the most important in ancient Egyptian history.

THE MIDDLE KINGDOM, 2040-1640

Mentuhotep II ruled for an incredible fifty-one years, long enough to heal the wounds of what was in essence a civil war between the Egyptians from Thebes and those from Herakleopolis. Soon after his victory, Mentuhotep added the title *Smatowy*, or The Unifier, to his name to signal the end of strife and the beginning of a new era. However, he realized that his real power depended on maintaining the support of the powerful nomarchs. He had led the war as the first among the nomarchs of Upper Egypt, and he quickly moved to replace the nomarchs of Lower Egypt with his fellow Thebans, whom he knew he could depend on. His rule was apparently benevolent, but it was also probably dependent on the goodwill of the nomarchs throughout Egypt.

Upon Mentuhotep's death, his son Mentuhotep III (2010–1998) became pharaoh and maintained the powerful state that his father had created. Like his father, he sent expeditions to Punt via the Red Sea to collect myrrh and other rare items. He carried on successful wars against the Bedouins in the Sinai, who threatened Egyptian mining interests, and built temples at Elephantine and Abydos to honor the god Osiris. Things began to change when Mentuhotep III died and was succeeded by his son Mentuhotep IV (1998–1991), who ruled for only seven years.

The most complete summary of the reign of Mentuhotep IV is on an extensive stone relief near the quarries at Wadi Hammamat. This sculpture shows the pharaoh about to drink a toast to the god Min, who protects Wadi Hammamat. An inscription on the relief states that the pharaoh has led ten thousand men to the site to cut stone for his sarcophagus, which is so heavy that three thousand men are needed to drag it away. Only the lid of this giant coffin survives, and judging by its size—13 feet (4m) wide by $6^{1}/_{2}$ feet (2m) long by 3 feet (1m) thick—it seems that the statement on the relief may have been true. The inscription also gives one important piece of historical data: Mentuhotep IV's second in command was Amenemhet, who on the relief is called "He Who Supervises Everything in the World."

loot. Wasting no time, Senwosret II drove the Libyans into the deep desert and set to work. The project was not finished when he died, but his son, Senwosret III (1878–1843), and grandson, Amenemhet III (1842–1797), continued the work, so that by about 1830 there was a 27-mile (43km) dam that created 153,600 acres (62,200ha) of fertile land for planting.

Senwosret II's foreign affairs were nearly as important as his domestic policies. During his reign, Egypt enjoyed profitable trade relations with Byblos, on the coast of Lebanon, as well as with the western Asian cities of Gaza and Megiddo in Palestine, Ugarit in Syria, and even Greek cities on the Aegean. Such foreign trade appears to have been conducted without any hint of violence or intimidation on either side. These mutually profitable trade relations continued throughout the Twelfth Dynasty, reaching a high point during the reign of Senwosret III; numerous eastern Mediterranean archaeological sites dating to this era reveal trade goods brought back home to western Asia by Mesopotamian, Assyrian, and Mycenaean traders from Egypt.

We can see evidence of one such trade encounter from the tomb paintings of the sixteen nomarchs whose tombs are at Beni Hasan, on the east bank of the Nile about 55 miles (90km) south of el-Fayum. These tombs are decorated with what were once brightly painted scenes out of the lives of Middle Kingdom nobles. One of them, from the tomb of Thuthotep, who ruled the Hare Nome of Upper Egypt around 1860, depicts the nomarch and his wife entertaining the

Bedouin prince Abshai and his entourage. Abshai is returning home from a successful trading venture in which he has traded galena to another nomarch, Khnumhotep, who ruled the nome next to Hare. The Egyptians prized galena as an eye makeup and traded finished goods for it. In the garden of Thuthotep, the Bedouin chief enjoys good food, wine, gracious gifts, and various entertainments, including acrobats and wrestling competitions.

Wrestling was a popular entertainment during the Middle Kingdom, and in another tomb dating to this period there is a contemporary scene of wrestlers engaged in a match. This artwork is truly unique, for it includes 140 smaller paintings, arranged sequentially in six rows, which illustrate a wrestling match between an Egyptian and a Nubian. Starting with a painting that shows the men facing each other, the sequence moves through the entire match as if one had isolated individual frames from a movie. The contrast of the black body of the Nubian and the lighter body of the

Egyptian makes it possible to observe and study every hold and grip of the athletes.

Senwosret I, also noted as a builder, ordered the construction of temples all over the Nile Valley. He rebuilt the Sun Temple at Heliopolis around 1968, and also erected a temple to Osiris at Karnak that contained a colossal 16-foot (5m) statue of the god. Unfortunately, almost none of Senwosret's architectural works have survived; they were simply torn down to be reused by later pharaohs. For instance, when Amenhotep III (1391–1353), a mighty builder in the New Kingdom period (1552–1085), built his temple at Karnak, he tore down and used the stones of Senwosret's temple to Osiris for a base. In A.D. 1930, however, Egyptologists turned the tables on Amenhotep and removed the stones from his pylon to rebuild Senwosret's temple to Osiris. Unfortunately, there was no such luck with his temple at Heliopolis. The site was only a few miles from modern Cairo and medieval Arabs stripped the site almost bare of stone for their own building purposes. Only a single obelisk survives of this once huge structure.

Amenemhet II and Senwosret II

Senwosret's son and grandson, Amenemhet II (1929–1895) and Senwosret II (1897–1878)—who, following Amenemhet I's precedent, ruled jointly from 1897 to 1895—continued the work that Senwosret started. Both leaders devoted a considerable amount of money to completing the great irrigation project in the Fayum. Part of this activity involved raising the status of Shedet, the capital of the Fayum.

Previously, Shedet had been a small, provincial town whose people worshipped a local crocodile god named Sebek. However, if the royal treasury was going to lavish wealth and labor on the Fayum project, it was necessary to elevate both the town and its god. By the reign of Amenemhet II, therefore, Sebek had become a manifestation of the Sun god Re known officially as Sebek Re, and Shedet was renamed Crocodilopolis. From then on, Sebek was pictured as a crocodile-headed man who wore both a sun disk, signifying that he was the sun god, and a cobra, which symbolized his status as a royal god of Lower Egypt. In the new mythology that followed, his mother was Neith, also the mother of Re.

In addition to continuing the project started at el-Fayum by his father and grandfather, Senwosret II sponsored an impressive engineering project of his own at the Second Cataract. Cataracts are waterfalls created by large expanses of rock, in this case granite, in a riverbed. They are generally serious impediments to navigation. It is difficult for ships to sail past these obstacles, especially large cargo vessels such as were necessary to supply the fortresses south of the Second Cataract. Ships often had to be drawn out of the water below a cataract, hauled overland, and then set back in the water above it. To address this problem, Senwosret ordered his engineers to hack a canal through solid granite that would be wide enough and deep enough for a loaded ship. This innovation allowed the Egyptians to more easily continue their expansion to the south along the course of the Nile. By the end of the reign of Senwosret's grandson, Amenemhet III (1842–1797), there were fourteen major fortresses extending south to beyond the Second Cataract.

But Senwosret II's construction plans did not stop there. The leader also built a typical Middle Kingdom pyramid at Lahun, near the Fayum; he surrounded a natural rock outcropping with retaining walls and filled the space between with mud rubble,

then covered everything over with limestone. There were, however, two things that made his burial place unique, both discovered by the famous British archaeologist Sir Flinders Petrie during excavations in 1891. One was a shaft tomb on the south side of the pyramid that held the magnificent jewelry of the royal princess Sithathoriunut (see pages 92-93). The other was a box marked with the pharaoh's seals which contained a five-month-old infant. The child was probably intended as a foundation offering to ensure the stability of the pyramid. If that was its purpose, it failed, for Rameses II's (1290–1224) builders stripped Senwosret's pyramid of its limestone. Without its protective covering, wind and rain eroded the core into a mound of rubble.

Senwosret III and Amenemhet III

The reign of Senwosret III (1878–1843) and that of his son Amenemhet III (1842–1797) represent the high point of the Middle Kingdom. These two kings were able to break the power of the nomarchs, remove them from positions of responsibility, and replace them as governmental administrators with members of the Egyptian middle class.

Since the reign of Amenemhet I, the power of the nomarchs had grown. For instance, Khnumhotep, ruler of the Oryx Nome, had a personal army of four hundred troops, which was apparently a particularly impressive number as it is mentioned prominently in Khnumhotep's tomb paintings. His neighbor Thuthotep

Above: This relief of the crocodile god Sebek seated on a throne and wearing the crown of Amun is from a late Egyptian temple (second century B.C.) at Kom Ombo, but similar reliefs were common in the Middle Kingdom period.

had been able to commission an alabaster statue of himself that was 22 feet (6.7m) tall, 6 feet (1.8m) taller than the one his pharaoh, Senwosret III, had commissioned for himself. Evidence of such personal power suddenly stops, however, in the middle of this pharaoh's reign. The means by which Senwosret III reasserted central power remain unknown, but historians can infer that it happened because once-powerful nomarchs like Khnumhotep were no longer able to construct large and elaborately furnished tombs, and the names of the new court officials who built their tombs beside that of Senwosret III were not the old family names of nomarchs, but those of new, previously unheard of men.

Senwosret III also moved quickly to reduce the influence of the nomes as governmental units. While the original forty-two nomes survived as traditional regions, the actual government was divided among three departments that in turn sectioned the country into three parts: the Delta; the area between Memphis and Thebes; and the land from Thebes to the border with Nubia. Within each of these three departments, the functions of government were split between four individuals: one in charge of administering the law, another to manage agriculture, a third to handle finances, and a fourth to handle overall administration. The control of all three departments was in the hands of the vizier, who in turn was directly responsible to the pharaoh.

The new organization and the elimination of the nomarchs made Senwosret III and his son Amenemhet III the most powerful rulers of the Twelfth Dynasty. For the first and only time during this dynasty an Egyptian army campaigned in Syria. A small mortuary statue of an official named Khusobek found at Abydos bears an inscription stating that

Khusobek accompanied the pharaoh on a campaign against a town called Sekmem. Although the town itself has not been identified, the inscription does state that it was in Retenu, the Egyptian designation for Syria. This is the only record of a Middle Kingdom pharaoh campaigning in this region. Perhaps in relation to that campaign, Senwosret rebuilt the fortifications at the edge of the Delta's border with Palestine.

In the south, Senwosret III declared that the fortresses of Semna and Kumma, just north of the Second Cataract, marked his southern border, and he set up two stelae to mark the precise boundary. Both of these stelae were inscribed with statements that no Nubians except traders were allowed north of the fortresses. Both fortresses had permanent garrisons. South of this point, Egyptian influence was also strong. At the Third Cataract, some 150 miles (240km) south of the official border, there was a massive fortresslike structure that seems to have been an Egyptian trading station, although it may have housed Nubian agents of Egypt, not true Egyptians.

To support his activities to the south, Senwosret III determined to cut a large canal through the granite base at the First Cataract. Although the Fifth Dynasty pharaoh Unas had already cut such a canal at the First Cataract, it had apparently eroded away or was otherwise useless. Senwosret's cut was truly impressive, measuring 260 feet (79m) long, 34 feet (10m) wide, and 26 feet (8m) deep. With such a canal, even the largest freighters and warships could pass the First Cataract with a minimum of difficulty, thus assuring a dependable supply route for Egyptian forces operating in Nubia.

Through trade or warfare the wealth of Nubia poured into Egypt during Senwosret III's reign. Gold became so plentiful that its value dropped below that

of silver. There are signs that business flourished in this trading environment. To facilitate trade, the Egyptians began to use the weight of copper to designate the value of an article so that items were said to be equivalent to so many *debens* of copper. Although this is still a long way from coinage, it was the first step because it established a fixed value for metal that could be used to estimate the value of goods and services.

Domestically, Senwosret III and his son began a flurry of building activity; unfortunately, most of it has not survived the ages. Much of the destruction was deliberate, carried out on the orders of Rameses II, the great "ego" of the New Kingdom, who tore down the buildings of his predecessors to enhance his own reputation. Records indicate, however, that Senwosret III and Amenemhet III built temples at Thebes, Edfu, Heliopolis, and Herakleopolis. At Abydos, the traditional home of the god Osiris, these pharaohs were

especially active, building a large temple with a wall around it where their favored officials were allowed to build tombs.

It is possible, based on presumptive evidence, that Senwosret III and Amenemhet III may have built the first canal connecting the Nile River with the Red Sea. The Greek geographer Strabo (64 B.C.–A.D. 24), along with Aristotle, in his *Meteorologica*, attributes such a canal to Senwosret, although Herodotus earlier claimed that the canal was built during the reign of Necho, between 672 and 664. If such a canal existed in the Middle Kingdom, it probably extended east from the Nile River near the Wadi Tumilat in the Delta to the Bitter Lakes or Lake Timsah, which may have been, at this early date, extensions of the Red Sea. Aerial photos of the area show embankments near modern Qantarah, which is near the Suez Canal. Certainly there are records from this period that prove that ships as large as 180 feet (55m) long did make voyages to the Red Sea port of Punt to trade for incense and gold.

The most important engineering feat of Senwosret III's and Amenemhet III's was the completion of the great irrigation project in the Fayum. It was Amenemhet who completed the great 27-mile (43km) dam that extended from Itsa to Biahmu. The pharaoh commemorated his great work by building at Biahmu two huge statues of himself—each nearly 60 feet (18m) tall—to mark the entrance to fertile Fayum.

Near these giant monoliths Amenemhet built a third commemorative structure, a huge complex that Herodotus

called the Labyrinth. This structure was both an administrative center and a temple. It measured 800 feet (244m) by 1,000 feet (305m) and had, according to Herodotus, three thousand different rooms—1,500 above ground and 1,500 below. There is a legend, recounted by Herodotus, that the Labyrinth was also a tomb for Amenemhet. According to this belief, the very size and complexity of the structure was intended to protect the king's body from tomb robbers. Herodotus writes that in his day the structure was still guarded by priests who allowed him free access to the rooms above ground, but forbade him to enter the subterranean rooms because they claimed one of them held the body of Amenemhet; many of the others, they said, were stuffed with the mummified bodies of thousands of

crocodiles, sacred to the memory of the crocodile god Sebek, who protected the Fayum.

However, Amenemhet might not have been entombed in the Labyrinth. Next to the Labyrinth is a 240-foot (73m) pyramid also built by Amenemhet III; the pharaoh may have been buried there. Like most pyramids of the Twelfth Dynasty, this edifice consists of a core of a naturally occurring rock covered with masonry rubble and faced with well fitted white limestone blocks. Unfortunately, the limestone was taken by succeeding generations of builders. With the casing eventually gone, the pyramid rapidly fell into ruins. Yet the interior of the pyramid survived to reveal a kind of mini-labyrinth within.

The path to the burial chamber is the most challenging of any pyramid in Egypt, according to Barbara Mertz, an Egyptologist who has studied it. The structure is filled with dead ends, and entrances to secret passages are concealed behind solid granite slabs that appear to be part of the ceilings or floors. The real burial chamber was cut out of one huge piece of granite, and its entrance was covered by a single rock weighing forty-five tons. Nevertheless, cunning ancient tomb robbers managed to find and enter this burial chamber, although it must have taken considerable time since archaeologists discovered dozens of tunnels, apparently chiseled by the robbers, that led nowhere. When these thieves finally found the true burial chamber, they looted everything and burned the mummy; Mertz believes that this was done as revenge for all the difficulty they had had to face.

LITERATURE OF THE MIDDLE KINGDOM

During the years of its ascendancy, the Twelfth Dynasty was a period of tremendous cultural, scientific, and artistic originality; in fact, some Egyptologists consider the 257 years of the Middle Kingdom to be Egypt's golden age. In their literature, sculpture, and jewelry making the Middle Kingdom was exceptional.

THE BOOK OF THE DEAD

Chief among the literary achievements of the Middle Kingdom was the development of *The Book of the Dead.* This well-known work evolved from the *Pyramid Texts* of the Old Kingdom, then added subject matter from the Coffin Texts of the First Intermediate Period. During the Old Kingdom, there developed a sophisticated collection of myths and guidelines governing the immortality of the pharaoh and his close associates. In The First Intermediate Period, the legend of Isis and Osiris became popular, and with it the idea that immortality was available to anyone who practiced certain rituals and lived a moral life in general.

During the Middle Kingdom, the myths governing immortality laid out specific actions and behaviors that Egyptians felt defined a moral life. Many of these new ideas are found in the coffin texts that continued to be written on the inside of wooden coffins, as they were during the First Intermediate Period. One of the chief emphases of these coffin texts are various descriptions of the multitude of monsters and evils that will threaten to destroy the *ka,* on its journey to Rosetau, the portal to the heavenly realm of Osiris. Only by reciting numerous charms and prayers can the *ka* successfully complete this dangerous journey.

As the Coffin Texts make clear, however, that is not the end of the *ka*'s problems. Once it has completed its journey, the *ka* must prove that it has lived a life that conforms to the dictates of Maat, often personified in the texts as a goddess wearing an ostrich feather on her head and holding an *ankh,* or symbol of life. But *maat* was also a collection of instructions that emphasized hard work, honesty, devotion to duty, piety, and acceptance of one's place in the world. These qualities largely determined who received the gift of eternal life. It was during the Middle Kingdom that the judging of how well one conformed to the dictates of *maat* became formalized.

Below: Scenes are painted on the inside of this wooden mummy case from the Twentieth Dynasty (first millenium B.C.). much as the Coffin Texts of the First Intermediate Period and Middle Kingdom were. These paintings show, among other things, the mummy of the deceased being prepared for burial.

judges, each of which presides over a particular sin. The soul must recite a list of thirty-six sins that he or she has not committed, and then must make a formal statement of innocence. Only then can the *ka* earn eternal bliss.

The Tale of Sinuhe

The literary efforts of the Middle Kingdom were not limited to works on the afterlife. This era also saw the production of dozens of adventure stories and poems, as well as legal texts, wills, and simple lists of people and supplies. The most famous piece of literature from the Middle Kingdom is the supposedly autobiographical account titled *The Tale of Sinuhe,* attributed to an Egyptian noble named Sinuhe who was an advisor to Amenemhet I. This story is important because it furthers our understanding of several things about Egypt at this time, including the Egyptian attitude toward foreigners, the awe in which the pharaoh was held, the Egyptian view of the dead, and even the political environment of the small states that sat on Egypt's borders.

The Tale of Sinuhe begins with Sinuhe's accompanying Amenemhet I's son Senwosret and his army on their return to Egypt from a successful campaign against the Libyans. Just as the army has set up camp at a point very close to the Delta region, word reaches Senwosret that his father, the pharaoh, has died. The text does not explain why, but something about the death terrifies Sinuhe. Perhaps he suspects that one of his relatives or friends at court was involved in this death. Whatever the reason, Sinuhe flees the camp in such a hurry that he takes no food, water, or supplies with him. He blindly runs into the desert and takes refuge behind two large bushes at the side of the road. When he decides it is safe to come out of hiding, he sneaks to the

Many coffin texts depict a judgment in the Hall of Maat where the *ka* of the deceased will be judged by Osiris, the god of the dead, and a panel of forty-two judges. The god Anubis leads the departed soul into the Hall of Maat, places the candidate before a scale, and then magically sets its heart in a dish on one end of a balance. At the other end of the balance is another dish with the ostrich feather of Maat in it. For a soul to gain the gift of immortality, the heart of the deceased must not outweigh the feather. Should this not happen, and the heart's weight causes the scale to dip, the offending *ka* is immediately seized and eaten by Ammit, the Devourer of Souls, a hideous creature with the head of a wolf. Ammit can often be seen in paintings and reliefs crouching near the scale, almost straining forward to watch it, anticipating the dip that will allow him to feed on the tainted soul.

Besides this fearsome exercise, the departed soul must make a statement to the panel of forty-two

west bank of the Nile, steals a boat, and floats across the river. From there he makes his way to the "Wall of the Prince," the fortified barrier that Amenemhet I had built to control Bedouin access to the Delta. He waits until dark to sneak past the watchful sentries.

Finally, Sinuhe makes his way into the desert, but having been without food for two days, he is weak from hunger. Luckily, he meets a Bedouin chieftain who had known him in better days. The Bedouin, who had apparently received a kindness from Sinuhe at some time in the past, takes the refugee to Nenshi, the ruler of Upper Retenu (probably part of modern Israel). Nenshi was apparently an ally of Egypt, for Sinuhe tells us that Egyptian was spoken at his court and there were a number of resident Egyptians there. These Egyptians tell Nenshi that Sinuhe had been a respected advisor to the pharaoh. Nenshi, pleased with these reports, recognizes Sinuhe as an asset and recruits him into his service. He was apparently not concerned with what Sinuhe had done in Egypt, nor with the reason he had fled. He even gives Sinuhe one of his daughters as a wife.

Nenshi offers Sinuhe the governorship of Yaa. This province was apparently located on the border between Retenu and Egypt, for Sinuhe states that travelers on their way to Egypt had to pass through it. But Yaa was also under constant threat of attack from Bedouins drawn to the place by its natural resources, which according to Sinuhe consisted of an abundance of figs, grapes, honey, and fruit and olive trees. Sinuhe describes Yaa as a land that is so rich that wine is more plentiful than water.

For many years Sinuhe led the armies of Nenshi against raiders; in these forays Sinuhe and his men brought back cattle, grain, and slaves. When his sons by his new wife were grown,

they also led troops against these marauders, with equal success. Once, however, Sinuhe was challenged to single combat by another noble in Nenshi's service. The prize was to be Sinuhe's lands. The event apparently became something of a cause célèbre, and a large number of the Retenuan population came to witness the fight. Both men were armed with axes, bows, javelins, and daggers. The "duel" began with an exchange of arrows. The challenger missed his shot, but Sinuhe shot an arrow through his enemy's neck. Thus disabled, the fellow was helpless, and Sinuhe proudly writes that he bashed in his head with the man's own ax. Afterward, Sinuhe consolidated his wealth—and thus enhanced his power—by confiscating his challenger's wealth.

It is interesting that Nenshi, as ruler of Retenu, does nothing to hinder the combat between two of his vassals. He favored Sinuhe, but apparently gave him only moral support.

Sinuhe could have spent his days in Retenu, gradually slipping into old age while his warrior sons held the territory for him. Yet he longed for his homeland. When he began to notice the hallmarks of

Below: Today, reproductions of this blue ceramic hippopotamus are among the most popular items in museum shops around the world. Actually, these hippos were produced in numerous other poses throughout the Middle Kingdom. This one dates from the Twelfth Dynasty.

old age—poor vision, flabby arms, and weak legs—he wrote a letter to the wife of the pharaoh begging her to intercede with her husband on his behalf so that he might return to Egypt and be buried in his native soil. We do not know the relationship between Sinuhe and Senwosret I's wife, but the lady—along with her children, who were also fond of Sinuhe—did as Sinuhe had asked. The pharaoh wrote his father's former advisor a letter giving him permission to return. In his story Sinuhe preserved the wording of the royal pardon. Whatever the problem had been, so many years before, the pharaoh says, is forgotten. In fact Senwosret claims not to know what caused Sinuhe to flee in the first place. He writes that both the queen and their children have been Sinuhe's stalwart supporters.

The pharaoh even offers Sinuhe a tomb fitted out at royal expense—the ultimate bribe for an Egyptian. Senwosret describes to Sinuhe the burial ceremony he can expect on his death; a gold mummy case with lapis lazuli inlay, an impressive funeral procession with oxen dragging the sarcophagus on a sledge, and official mourners wailing behind. At Sinuhe's own funeral chapel, the priests will perform all the right ceremonies, including prayers and animal sacrifices. Surely, Senwosret writes, this is better than being wrapped in a dusty sheep skin and dumped into some hole in the ground, as is the custom in Retenu.

Sinuhe immediately turns his province over to his sons and sends an acceptance letter back to the pharaoh. He makes his way to an Egyptian border post where he finds that the pharaoh has sent ships with luxuries and supplies to welcome him. Arriving at the royal palace, Sinuhe is admitted to the royal presence and throws himself full length and face down on the floor, in the traditional manner of approaching the pharaoh. He is so overcome that when, on the

pharaoh's orders, guards raise him from the floor and the pharaoh orders him to speak, he cannot. Prompted by the pharaoh, he stammers out his thanks and is greeted by the queen and her children, who, at first, do not recognize this uncouth stranger with his foreign beard and barbaric clothing.

The story closes with Sinuhe's describing his new tomb, with its furnishings and front garden. He is especially thrilled that the tomb is within the sacred precinct of the pharaoh's own pyramid and near the tomb of the queen.

The Tale of Sinuhe has at least two levels of meaning. First, it is a classic tale of adventure. An innocent victim of circumstances falls from favor yet nevertheless makes the best of things, rising to new successes until his merits are recognized by those above him and he is called back to assume his rightful place at court. Secondly, it is a propaganda piece written to extol the wisdom and kindness of Senwosret I. We never really learn why Sinuhe had to flee. Probably, the author of the tale was writing for an audience that already knew the particulars of Sinuhe's misfortunes. The story is too detailed in its other particulars for the cause of all his misfortunes to be omitted unless it was common knowledge.

The real point of the story is that Sinuhe's situation gives Senwosret the chance to be magnanimous and forgiving, as a pharaoh should be. Once the pharaoh learned the facts of Sinuhe's foreign successes and heard the petition of the queen and her children, he takes the initiative and asks Sinuhe to come home—not just a simple, grudging permission, but almost a royal supplication for a dear and faithful follower to return. Senwosret baits the invitation with things nearest and dearest to an Egyptian's heart—a splendid tomb near the pharaoh's.

In the end, the story reflects well on Sinuhe, of course, but it also gave ancient readers an example of the kinds of things that could happen to a faithful servant of the pharaoh. No doubt this picture was part of the reason why the story was so popular in ancient Egypt. It was the standard literary piece that young student scribes used to practice penmanship; therefore, the tale was widely circulated among that literate segment of Egyptian society from which the pharaoh's servants would come.

JEWELRY OF THE MIDDLE KINGDOM

The Middle Kingdom has justly been typified by Egyptologists as a golden age of literature in Egypt. No less impressive, on a purely artistic level, is the jewelry of the period. Middle Kingdom Egyptians loved jewelry, not only because it enhanced their appearance and advertised their wealth but also because they believed that jewelry had magical and protective qualities. Jewelry in the shape of birds, for instance, was supposed to protect the wearer from snakes and scorpions since birds both preyed on these creatures and gave warnings with their cries when they were nearby. And the quest for immortality might be enhanced by possession of jewelry in the shape of a scarab. Scarabs were copies of dung beetles, and in Egypt this insect collected excrement, rolled it into little balls, and then pushed these balls to a nest where they served both as a food source and an incubator for beetle eggs. The Egyptians had observed that new beetles emerged from this most fundamental type of matter, and they felt this was a miracle. To possess a scarab—a model beetle—was magical insurance of a person's immortality.

The Egyptians also used jewelry in the shape of body parts such as arms, legs, and eyes. These were to confer protection against ailments in those particular limbs or organs.

Jewelry also advertised status and power, much as it does today. The pharaoh and his family set the standard in this realm, and the rest of Egypt followed. Of course, the royal family's body decorations were more elaborate and more expensive than those of anyone else, but to a large degree Egyptians copied the styles of the royal family in less expensive versions—while the royal family used semiprecious stones, the rest of Egypt was content with facsimiles made of paste.

The popularity of jewelry during the Middle Kingdom was possible because of the ready availability of gold and semiprecious gems such as carnelian, jasper, garnet, amethyst, rock crystal, obsidian, and

turquoise. Egyptian jewelers had access to lapis lazuli and silver through well-established trade connections with Nubia, Mesopotamia, and even western India.

Middle Kingdom jewelers created their pieces with the simplest of tools. Bronze and copper were the only metals available to make hammers, tongs, and picks, while sandstone and quartzite served to smooth and polish. To perforate stones, Egyptian jewelers used a bow drill tipped with flint. The only furnaces available were small charcoal ovens made of pottery, in which the jeweler regulated the heat by blowing through a clay-tipped reed. It was not until the New Kingdom (1552–1085) that the bellows was designed to create more intense heat. Despite the primitive nature of their tools, the Egyptians were able to create masterpieces.

A representative collection of Middle Kingdom royal jewelry that still dazzles observers are the necklaces, bracelets, and pectoral piece of the Princess Sithathoriunut, daughter of Senwosret II and wife of Amenemhet III, her nephew. Archaeologists discovered this hoard tucked away in a recess of her tomb that was at the bottom of a shaft on the south side of Senwosret II's pyramid at Lahun. We will never know why Sithathoriunut chose to be buried here, rather than near her husband's tomb at Hawara, but we are lucky that the jewels escaped the notice of tomb robbers. When Sir Flinders Petrie excavated the tomb in A.D. 1914, he found only a few scattered bones; the ancient tomb robbers apparently had torn the mummy apart in a search for treasure that was often placed within the lengths of linen wrapping used in the mummification process. The robbers were perhaps fooled by the cheap paste imitations of jewels that were placed with the corpse and so missed the real jewels that lay hidden in the wall.

The cache consisted of a golden head band decorated with a cobra that sat above the middle of the forehead and fifteen evenly spaced rosettes, each decorated with a feather design around a cross. Two golden bands hung down from the gold band on either side of the princess' head in line with her ears. Thin bands of gold that apparently were not attached to this head-piece were also among the treasure, but these may have been entwined through the hair of the wig that the princess wore.

The most spectacular piece in this group was a large trapezoidal pectoral that was designed to hang around Sithathoriunut's neck on a cord consisting of teardrop-shaped beads of turquoise, carnelian, gold, and obsidian. This pectoral bore the cartouche of Senwosret II supported by a crouching figure of a man and framed between two falcons executed in cloisonné with pieces of turquoise and carnelian.

The princess' treasure also included two bracelets decorated with rows of carnelian, turquoise, gold, and lapis lazuli, and a number of necklaces made of cowry shells. In addition to the jewelry, a number of toilet items were found in the cache. These included a silver mirror with an obsidian handle in the shape of the goddess Hathor decorated with the usual gold, lapis lazuli, crystal, and carnelian; perfume jars made of obsidian; and golden-handled copper knives and razors, as well as two whetstones to sharpen them.

There were also alabaster ointment pots for kohl and skin oils. Kohl, used as an eyeshadow, was made from a variety of minerals, depending on the desired color—malachite, for instance, made green eyeshadow and galena made gray. These minerals were ground on slate palettes and stored in tiny jars. Although Egyptians used kohl to enhance the beauty of the eyes, they also considered it a medicinal aid against trachoma, an infectious eye disease that was prevalent in ancient Egypt. Eye shadow would also be useful for decreasing glare in the bright desert sunlight.

The princess' ointment jars probably also contained skin oils to soften and protect the skin from the drying effects of the desert climate. From the beginning of the Old Kingdom period, Egyptian cosmetologists had pressed oils from fruits and olives as well as from flowers and herbs, mixing them with animal fat to make compounds to soften and protect the skin.

Royal users of such jewelry and beauty aids were trendsetters for the rest of Egypt. In the excavations of village sites near the great tomb complexes of the Middle Kingdom, archaeologists have unearthed numerous cheap imitations of the type of jewelry worn by Sithathoriunut. At Kahun, a village for workers who built the pyramids and tombs of the era's royalty, excavators found not only cosmetic pots and toilet articles similar to those owned by the princess, but also copies in wood of the Hathor handle that was part of the princess' silver mirror. Whereas jewelry of a royal princess would be made of gold and semiprecious stones, copies of royal pieces contained a more common grade of amethyst, garnet, and quartz. Pottery with distinctively bright green or blue glazes was also sometimes used in the imitations.

Middle Kingdom art also includes some distinctive sculpture, for this was the only time in the long history of Egyptian art that artists escaped from a stiff, impersonal style of depicting pharaohs, their wives, and the nobility. Old Kingdom sculpture faithfully represented the actual appearance of the people depicted, but the faces were always distant and aloof—more godlike than human. In the Middle Kingdom, however, portraitists occasionally attempted to depict emotion. The portrait sculptures of Amenemhet II and Senwosret III now in the Metropolitan Museum in New York, and another statue of Senwosret III now in the Louvre, all depict men with worried, one might even say despondent, facial expressions. The Louvre statue shows a frowning Senwosret with especially heavy eyelids and huge ears almost certainly sculpted from life. This is the first time that Egyptian art portrays anything uncomplimentary in a pharaoh's portrait. Strangely, while the faces are realistically depicted, the bodies of the statues are the usual representation of strong virile young men. They do not really match the care-worn faces.

Below: A wooden model of a woman's head emphasizes the fact that stylish Egyptians had shaved heads under their elaborate wigs. The head is from el-Lisht, the necropolis area for the Middle Kingdom capital of Itjtawy.

SCIENCE AND MEDICINE IN THE MIDDLE KINGDOM

The Middle Kingdom also featured great advances in science and medicine. Most of the medical texts that survive from ancient Egypt seem to have been written during this period, although most of those exist only in later New Kingdom copies. One medical text that does survive in a Middle Kingdom version is the famous Kahun Papyrus. This document, written about 1825, was devoted exclusively to the medical problems of women. The recognition of medicine for women as a deserving specialty marks a definite advance in the history of medicine. However, it is mitigated by the fact that, by and large, the cures and treatments are largely ineffective by modern standards.

The best example of that ineffectiveness is clear from the portions of the Kahun Papyrus that deal with predicting whether a woman is pregnant and what the sex of her baby will be. This process involves having a woman urinate into a dish of emmer wheat and also into a dish of barley. If, after several days, the barley sprouts, the woman will have a boy. If, however, the emmer wheat sprouts, she will bear a girl. If neither grows, she is not pregnant. Another test for pregnancy involved inserting an onion in the woman's vagina when she went to sleep. If she had the smell of onion on her breath the next morning, she was pregnant.

The Kahun Papyrus also considers contraception. According to one method, a suppository could be made of mashed crocodile dung mixed with fermented bread dough and placed in the vagina. Another suggestion involved soaking mashed camel dung in vinegar and inserting that into the vagina. The effectiveness of either method is questionable, although one investigator, Emil Frey, has recently suggested that crocodile dung mixed with fermented dough might raise the pH level enough to prevent conception. Other modern writers suggest, however, that the presence of a mass of crocodile or camel dung in the vagina would prevent conception only by decreasing the ardor of the male. One last suggestion for contraception involves inserting nearly a pint of honey mixed with sodium carbonate or saltpeter into the vagina. Such a large amount of honey would probably act as a barrier to the sperm, but little else.

Then as now, women feared the effects of aging on their appearance. The Kahun Papyrus recommends that to prolong the youthful appearance of the breasts, a woman should smear them with the menstrual blood of a young woman, one who had just started to menstruate.

Finally, there are a number of passages in the papyrus that deal with specific female ailments. Some investigators believe that one passage records the first diagnosis of cervical cancer. The primary symptom is described as a smell of burnt flesh emanating from the vagina, and it is suggested that this is caused by the misalignment of the womb within the woman's body. The recommended cure is to burn frankincense and oil underneath the woman as she stands with spread legs so that the smoke will bring the womb back into correct alignment. This is an attempt at what anthropologists call sympathetic magic, whereby a problem is rectified by reproducing elements of the symptom externally in an effort to achieve a balance.

EVERYDAY LIFE IN THE MIDDLE KINGDOM

While the Middle Kingdom is justly famous for the literary and artistic gems it produced, it is also renowned for a wealth of mundane artifacts that Egyptologists have used to gain insight into the everyday life of Egyptian commoners. Such material comes from the famous site at Kahun, a town built around 1895 by the architect of Senwosret II's pyramid, Anpy, to house the monument's workers. After the pyramid was completed, a comparatively large number of workers stayed on to staff the temples that were part of any pharaoh's funeral site.

Kahun lies to the east of the Bahr Yusuf, the river that joins the Fayum to the Nile. It is only a little over a mile from the pyramids at Lahun and is situated near the northern end of the great dike that regulated the inflow and outflow of water to the Fayum's lake. In ancient times, the town was called Hetep-Senwosret, or Senwosret Is Happy, and included two distinct and separate areas. The first area featured a royal residence to house the visiting pharaoh, along with nine luxury houses where the directors of the site lived. The second area included more than one hundred far more modest homes which housed the common workers and craftsmen who performed the backbreaking labor of tomb building.

Kahun was specially located to be isolated. This is understandable since ancient Kahun was home to a select, highly skilled group of men and women who not only had an intimate knowledge about the secrets of the tombs, but also worked with precious and rare commodities. The whole site was surrounded with a mud brick wall and was constructed so that there were only two entrances in or out of the workers' quarters. The layout of the streets in this "blue collar" area was such that one watchman could easily observe all the comings and goings. The workers' quarters formed the western third of Kahun, while the eastern two thirds of the town, the "high-rent district," was separated from the workers' area by a high, thick wall.

The palace of the pharaoh, which excavators later called the Acropolis, sat at the top of a high platform of earth held in place behind a large stone retaining wall. The Acropolis was so high that from it one could look over the roofs of every house in the town. Although little remains of the building, it appears to have had high ceilings supported by pillars and a number of rooms, built with open roofs around pools of water, that served as both living quarters and reception areas. The whole impression was that here was a place of elegant repose where a pharaoh and his family could supervise the building of their eternal homes.

HOUSING

On the north and south wall of the "upper class" section were nine dwellings of considerable size—137 feet by 197 feet (42×60m)—that obviously housed some important people. The main doorway of each opened onto a foyer that in turn had three doorways, each of which led to a different section of the house. The one at left led to the offices of the important personage who supervised some aspect of the construction at Lahun. The central one led to a large area open to the sky that was surrounded by a colonnaded porch on all four sides; this space was surely, at one time, a formal garden where an important man might hold official receptions or entertain his equals. And the door at right led to private lodging for the family, which also had an open court with a large pool in the center. Like the room reached through the central doorway, this area had colonnades on all four sides. At the rear of this structure, behind the office, garden, and family section, were rooms where the servants who ran the house lived and worked. A small section behind the family area may have been the harem area.

Each of these nine houses was a carbon copy of the others. The floor plan, the design of the pillars, the color of the walls, and the design of the doorways were all exactly the same; the houses give every indication that they were built at the same time by the same person, according to one master plan to house the families of the main administrators of the Lahun complex.

This homogenized architectural plan is all the more obvious when one crosses the wall into the workers' area and finds eleven streets lined on both sides with houses that are all based on exactly the same design. With few exceptions, one entered each five-room house through an arched doorway with a wooden frame and a heavy plank door, fitted with a bolt for security, that led to an entryway or foyer. The foyer often had a small religious shrine to a particular god built into the left-hand wall. The inhabitants of Kahun worshipped several different gods at these shrines, but the most popular seem to have been Tauret, goddess of childbirth; Soped, god of the Sinai trade routes; Hathor, goddess of agriculture; and Sebek, the local crocodile god. The shrine consisted of a small pillar with a bowl on top, in which a member of the family would place a small amount of bread or bread dough

each day. Egyptians were too practical to leave good food at the shrine, so after an hour or two the offering was generally removed and eaten.

Behind the foyer was the large general living room where the family carried on most of its indoor activities. The ceiling of this room was higher than that of any other room in the house, which made its upper walls project above the rooms on either side. Windows that cut through these walls looked out onto the roofs of the other rooms and formed a clerestory that admitted light. Next to this large room was a bedroom and a hall leading to the kitchen in the back of the house. The kitchen had a domed clay oven for cooking set in one corner and a natural stone-lined depression set into the center of the floor for grinding grain into flour. At the very back of the house, dug into the ground, was a cellar where food and supplies were stored.

Usually, a stairway between two rooms led to the roof, although occasionally the stairway might be on the outside of the house. The roof of every room except the kitchen was made of beams set in the walls and covered with long poles laid crosswise over the beams. They were then covered with a layer of straw covered with mud. Some of the houses at Kahun had roofs that were supported by arches. In any event, the roofs had to be strong because the Egyptians were an outdoor people who spent much of their time at home on their roofs. Since each house was built close to the next and often shared a common wall with the dwelling next door, the roofs became the major social area in an Egyptian town, where men visited with each other at the end of the workday and women chatted together during the day while they carried on household chores. The roof over the kitchen was usually not covered with a layer of mud, but with only a layer of straw and twigs, to let the smoke from the cooking fires escape.

Excavations at Kahun have revealed that the furnishings of these workingmen's houses were very simple in design and usually consisted of beds, chests, and tables. Many houses did not have benches or other seating, and the family sat on the floor. The beds had a distinctive type of pillow consisting of a concave piece of wood set atop a two- or three-inch (5–7.5cm) stick glued into a wooden base. This shape may strike the modern observer as terribly uncomfortable, but the Egyptians felt that this kept the head elevated at a comfortable level and offered some protection against

scorpion bites, which were especially dangerous above the neck. Egyptians felt that the fabric pillows used in foreign nations were unhygienic.

The walls of the rooms were uniformly covered with white plaster and decorated with a series of strips and borders. Just above the floor, all four walls were painted with a dark color. About three or four feet (1–1.3m) above that strip, a black line a few inches thick was painted just below a red line of the same thickness. From the top of the red line to the ceiling, the wall was painted a dull yellow.

Below: Although this Egyptian "pillow" is an elaborate one made of ivory from the New Kingdom tomb of Tutankhamun, it is similar to pillows from throughout Egyptian history.

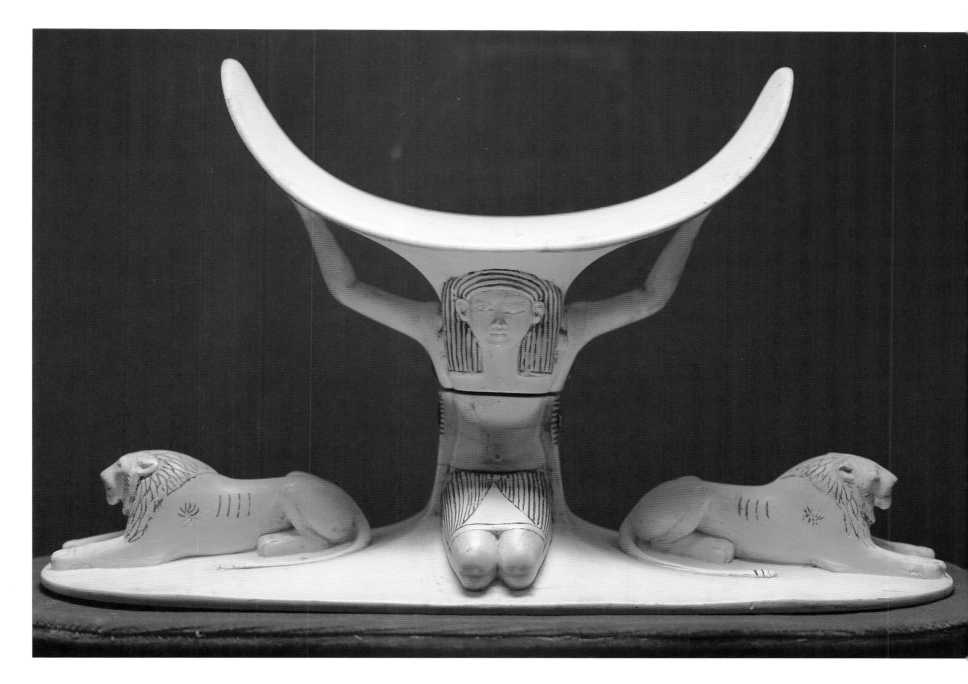

Above: A tomb painting of the nobleman Ity from the First Intermediate period shows workers transporting grain and storing it, as well as a group of wild ibexes. Although it is not from the Middle Kingdom, it represents the type of agricultural activity practiced during the period.

Food

Archaeologists have also uncovered remnants of the food eaten by the people of Kahun. Theirs was a healthy diet but a boring one. The main items were bread and beer, both of which were made in the traditional manner used by people of the Old Kingdom. To these staples the Egyptians added fish, beans, onions, and cucumbers. Beef was a delicacy that formed a staple only for those at the top levels of Egyptian society. Simple farmers and craftspeople seldom had the opportunity to eat it. The reason was simple: cattle required grass to eat, and grass had to compete with other crops on the small amount of fertile land along the Nile.

During the Middle Kingdom, wine—made by the Egyptians from grapes, dates, pomegranates, and palms—was becoming more popular. By the end of the era, the upper classes were beginning to import special vintages from Asia. Wine was stored in long pottery amphoras with resin-coated insides. The top of each amphora was capped with a clay stopper that was vented to prevent the fermentation gases from blowing it off.

Clothing

Both rich and poor of Egypt dressed in linen made from the flax plant. The quality of the linen, rather than the cut and design, was what differentiated rich from poor. The coarser linen was worn by the lower classes and the finest, sheerest linen was worn by the upper classes. The cleanliness of the cloth also advertised a person's social rank, since in a country without soap "doing the laundry" was a task that required either lots of time or a number of servants. The general method of cleaning involved soaking the linen in water, beating it with a board or rock to remove dirt, rinsing it, then letting it dry in the sun. The linen clothing of the wealthy often had pleats that were pressed into the fabric by placing the garments in wooden forms and letting them dry in the sun.

Most people in ancient Egypt went barefoot and saved sandals, which were generally made of papyrus fibers, only for special occasions. It was customary even among the wealthy to carry their sandals to a destination before putting them on.

The Life of Women

Perhaps the most important find at Kahun, as far as learning about the everyday life of ancient Egypt, was the discovery of thousands of pieces of papyruses that, when assembled and translated, revealed a great deal about the legal system, marriage and divorce customs, work patterns, and government. These records are some of the earliest written information about people other than the elite.

The marriage contracts and wills are especially revealing about the place of women in Middle Kingdom society. The overall impression drawn from these documents is that Egyptian women enjoyed a much higher status than any other group of women in the ancient world. This is especially true of the upper class, where wives often acted as spokespersons and conducted business for their absent husbands.

Women brought their own property to a marital union and continued throughout the marriage to exercise control over it, unless there was a formal transfer, in writing, at the beginning of the marriage, to the husband. If there was a divorce, the law dictated that a woman be able to take the property she had brought to the marriage. Some contracts even stipulated that, in the event of a divorce, the husband had to give the wife twice the value of what she had brought. These marriage contracts were quite detailed and specific, listing, for instance, the specific items, such as pots, pans, utensils, grain, or farm animals, that the woman owned. The details were worked out between the woman's father and husband-to-be, and the woman's father kept the document in his possession.

We learn from documents like these that girls married at the onset of puberty, which for ancient Egyptians seemed to be between ages twelve and fifteen. Most marriages were monogamous, although polygyny was an option for men who were wealthy enough to afford more than one wife. It is also clear, contrary to the popular modern notion, that marriages between full brothers and sisters were extremely rare until Ptolemaic times (332–31). Until that time, the comparatively small number of brother-sister marriages were between half-brothers and half-sisters, specifically between children of the same father but different mothers. Most of these marriages were among members of the royal family and were intended to ensure the legitimacy of the royal line.

Outside of the nobility, where marriages were often political alliances, it seems that most Egyptian young people enjoyed the freedom to pick their own husbands and wives as long as they chose men and women within their own classes. Letters and other documents make it clear that romantic love was an expected consequence of marriage. The husband's family, with whom the young couple went to live, received the bride into the family group with the same affection they would be expected to show a blood child. In fact the word "sister," strange as it sounds to modern ears, was used in place of the word "wife" to signify the love that the family held for the bride.

Certainly in one regard, ancient Egyptian women were much better off than their modern contemporaries, for there is no evidence that the ancient Egyptians practiced female circumcision—a process that nearly 80 percent of modern Egyptian girls undergo despite its official ban by the Egyptian government.

Besides comparative freedom to contract whatever marriage pleased them, Egyptian women had the right to conduct their own business ventures completely independent of their husbands or fathers. Sometimes this freedom was exercised in the extreme, for there are records from Kahun indicating that on at least one occasion a daughter sued her father.

Records also show that women worked alongside men in certain industries such as commercial bakeries, breweries, and weaving shops. Weaving cloth was exclusively a woman's job, but men in the same factory were responsible for spinning the yarn. Some jobs that are often considered woman's work were exclusively male. For instance, doing the laundry at the riverbank was men's work due to the potential threat of crocodiles.

Unlike in many ancient societies, in Egypt women were regularly provided for in their husbands' wills. A frequent distribution of property in wills was one third to the wife and two thirds to the children. If a wife predeceased her husband, and the wife had left a will, the provisions of that document were honored and her property distributed as she had directed.

We do not know how characteristic of the lives of the majority of Egyptians these documents were. The documents from Kahun record the details of the lives of people who were a specialized and privileged class of Middle Kingdom Egyptians. Even a common laborer at Kahun probably lived better than the vast majority of Egyptian peasants who made their living by farming along the banks of the Nile. Still, it does seem that the things that made life more pleasant—a neat house, a few luxuries, and a little leisure now and then—were available to a few more people than in the Old Kingdom. It is perhaps unfair to measure an ancient civilization by our own standards, but it does seem that at least some advances were made during the Middle Kingdom in terms of a better life for more people.

THE END OF THE MIDDLE KINGDOM

When Amenemhet III died after a reign of forty-five years, his son Amenemhet IV became pharaoh and continued the strong traditions of the Twelfth Dynasty for another twelve years (1844–1797). Although we know little about the details of his reign, the number of Egyptian manufactured goods that archaeologists have uncovered in Nubia, Syria, Palestine, and Crete suggest that Egypt's power and prestige continued for some time.

Yet there are signs that the power of the ruling family began to decline following this pharaoh's death. Amenemhet had no son, and so the throne went to his half-sister and wife, Sebeknefru, who ruled in her own right as pharaoh from 1787 to 1783. This was not unprecedented, for at least one female pharaoh had existed in the Old Kingdom. Most scholars believe that Egyptian society was matrilineal (that is, that families traced their lines through the female) and that occasionally, when there was no male heir, women had tra-

ditionally ascended to power. Regardless, Sebeknefru's social rank, as Amenemhet's queen, would have been so high that no one but another member of her family could have married her. If there was no such person, then marriage was impossible.

We know nothing about the four-year reign of Sebeknefru, because her tomb has not been found, but serious changes must have occurred during this period because when the record becomes clearer, a new dynasty is ruling Egypt; the pharaohs of this new dynasty are completely dominated by their viziers; northern Egypt is dominated by foreigners; and the country is experiencing periodic hardship due to fluctuations in the annual Nile flood. For the two centuries that followed, Egypt underwent a cultural, economic, and military slump.

Above: A painting from the tomb of the powerful nomarch Khnumhotep at Beni Hasan portrays workers gathering figs while three playful baboons sit in the tree eating fruit.

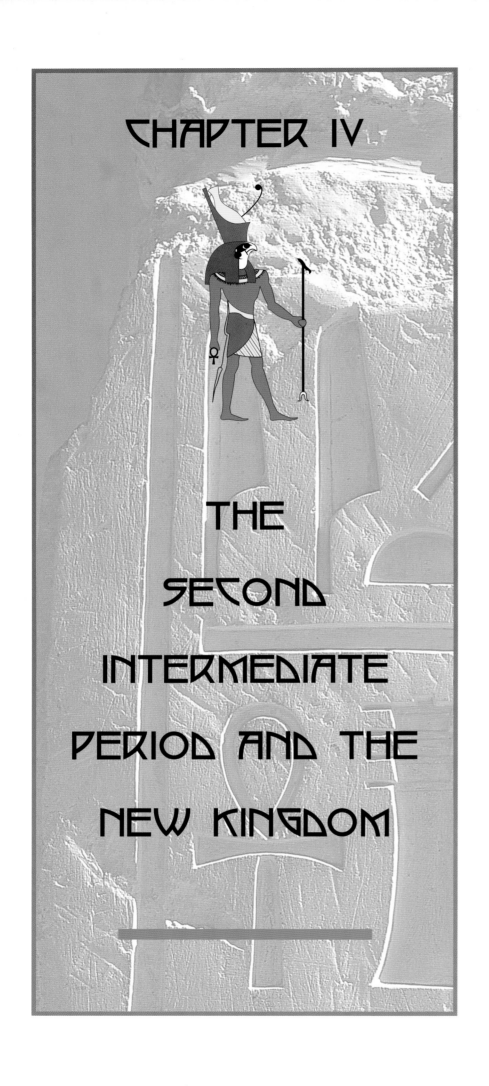

CHAPTER IV

THE

SECOND

INTERMEDIATE

PERIOD AND THE

NEW KINGDOM

EGYPT'S SECOND INTERMEDIATE PERIOD, 1783-1552

At the end of the Middle Kingdom, just as at the end of the Old Kingdom, there was a period of change brought about by the weakening of the central government, fluctuations in the annual Nile flood, and the invasion of foreigners—the Hyksos—into Egypt. Despite all this, the Second Intermediate Period, which is dated from 1783 to 1552, was not nearly as violent and chaotic as the First Intermediate Period had been. This is the judgment of modern-day Egyptologists whose analysis of the physical evidence and recently discovered written evidence reveals that, although there were changes in the government, the general pic-ture of Egyptian society at this time was one of order and stability.

But if a contemporary student of Egypt ignored the archaeological record and relied instead on the ancient written sources, such as *The History of Manetho* and the official statements of the New Kingdom pharaohs, such a student would come to believe that the Second Intermediate Period was a time when the Hyksos, brutal barbarians from southwest Asia, subjected Egypt and its people to a carnival of blood, rape, and pillage. Why does such a dichotomy exist between the opinion of contemporary investigators and that of the Egyptians who lived closer to the Second Intermediate Period?

The answer is propaganda. When the leaders of the Seventeenth Dynasty at Thebes went to war against the Hyksos living in the Delta region of Lower Egypt, they found it useful to motivate their people and to justify their attacks on the Delta by painting their enemies in the worst possible light. A victory, then, might seem like a miraculous delivery from foreign oppressors and a return to better times. It is probably the first recorded example of "the good old days" motif in history. In reality, the transition from the end of the Twelfth Dynasty, about 1783, to the Thirteenth Dynasty, and the subsequent rise to dominance of the Hyksos people in the Delta around 1640, was anything but chaotic.

THE THIRTEENTH DYNASTY

The Twelfth Dynasty had ended simply because of a lack of heirs. Queen Sebeknefru, who ruled as pharaoh from 1787 to 1783, died without heirs and was succeeded by Wegaf (1783–1779), the first representative of a family that would supply the seventy pharaohs of

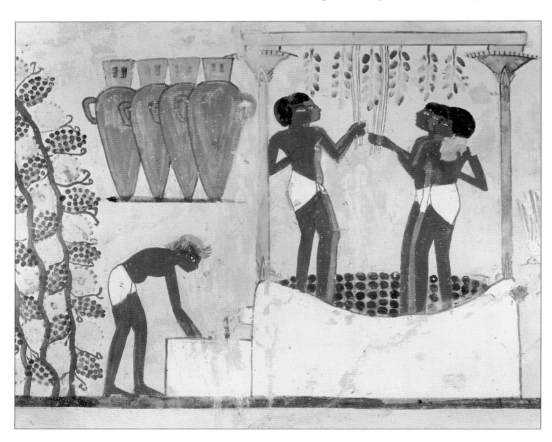

the Thirteenth Dynasty (1783–1640). The unique thing about these leaders is that they have left us almost nothing but their names. Archaeologists have been able to discover only a few of their tombs or temples, and these are poorly built or unfinished and overshadowed by the much more impressive remnants of the Middle Kingdom before them and the New Kingdom afterward.

The largest pyramid of the Thirteenth Dynasty is that of the Pharaoh Amenygemau, built around 1760 at Dahshur; this pyramid, measuring only 147 feet (45m) square at the base, is rather small and was never finished. Only one royal mummy from the Thirteenth Dynasty has been found—that of the pharaoh Hor (dates unknown), uncovered at Dahshur in a badly ruined pyramid. The tomb had of course been robbed. At Gebelein, north of Aswan, and at Nag el-Madamud,

just east of Luxor, stand the remains of temples built by the pharaohs Djedneferre, Dedumose II, Neferhotep III, Amenemhet VII, Sebekhotep II, and Sebekhotep III; but the ruins are so poorly preserved, because the temples were so badly built, that archaeologists have learned little from them. Even the dates of these leaders' reigns either are unknown or are approximations.

However, there is no evidence of the wholesale destruction and devastation that archaeologists usually find in a period of weak leadership in the ancient world. There continued to be a functioning government at Itjtawy, with a pharaoh at the apex and plenty of bureaucrats at work. Apparently, the governmental reforms of the Twelfth Dynasty pharaoh Senwosret III survived, and local officials continued to govern in the name of the pharaoh. It does appear, though, that the real power lay with the viziers, the advisors to the

Above: A row of columns in the courtyard on the island of Philae lead to the Temple of Isis. All the ruins of Philae had to be moved to another site when the Aswan Dam, the huge hydroelectric project on the Nile, was completed in the twentieth century A.D., several millenia after this temple was constructed.

Right: Sebek, the crocodile god, was one of the popular local deities who was also adopted by the foreigners who ruled Egypt, in this case the Ptolemies in the fourth through first centuries B.C.
Below: These two small figurines, each about four inches (10cm) tall, are Egyptian representations of a Black African and an Asian porter. The African figure is made of limestone, and the Asian of alabaster.

pharaohs who may have been the true rulers and who used the pharaohs as mere puppets.

In any case, there is no sign that Egypt weakened on her frontiers, for the borders in the Sinai and below the Second Cataract remained intact, with no evidence that they were breached by invaders.

Surprisingly, despite the periodic failure of the Nile flood to reach optimum levels for irrigation, some areas of Egypt enjoyed a moderate prosperity. The number of private tombs and temples actually increased, both in and around the great necropolises of the Middle and Old Kingdoms and at the new sites at Gebelein and Nag el-Madamud.

FOREIGNERS IN EGYPT

One change is apparent, however: a growing number of foreigners began to appear in the service of the government. Most of these were Asians from what is now

Israel and Jordan. Archaeology has revealed the presence of Asian artisans at Kahun during the Twelfth Dynasty. By the time of the Thirteenth Dynasty, the numbers of these foreigners had dramatically increased. One list of ninety-five household servants from the reign of Pharaoh Sebekhotep III, who flourished around 1745, included nearly forty-five names that are identifiably Asian or Semitic.

About 1640, a group of these Asians, whom the

fourth-century historian Manetho called Hyksos, arrived in force from the area that is now southern Israel. Manetho preserves the legend that they settled by force and ruled with a reign of terror, but there is no evidence to support the idea that they were especially brutal conquerors. In fact, they seem to have respected the Egyptian culture. Their leaders even adopted the Egyptian religion and called themselves pharaoh, taking Egyptian throne names along with their native ones.

From the records that survive, it seems that the Hyksos adopted the civilization of the Egyptians wholesale. They maintained the governmental structure that had grown out of the Twelfth Dynasty and lasted through the Thirteenth. In fact, they used native Egyptians to run the government. They adapted their Semitic gods to Egyptian gods, so that Baal became Seth, who was the brother of Osiris, and Astarte took on the characteristics of Seth's wife, Nephthys. They did not stop with worshipping the Egyptian gods, but identified their pharaohs as the earthly manifestations of Re, restored Egyptian temples, and imitated the religious art from the Middle Kingdom.

Despite centuries of speculation, we are still uncertain as to their ethnicity. Unfortunately, much confusion about the origins of these people comes from an early mistranslation of their name. The name Hyksos is a corruption of the Egyptian words *hikau khasut*, or "princes of the desert," but in the first century A.D. a Jewish historian named Josephus (A.D. 37/38–after 93/94) incorporated some of Manetho's material into his work and incorrectly translated the term *hikau khasut* as "captive shepherds." This mistranslation convinced generations of scholars that this was evidence of the presence of the ancient Jews in Egypt, where, after ruling for a time, they were conquered and turned into slaves—the same slaves that Moses subsequently freed. While the Hyksos may have been Semitic, there is no evidence to connect them with the Jews of Moses' era. More likely, according to recent research, they were Hurrians from Syria and Amorites, whom the Bible calls Canaanites.

Despite this remaining question, and even though they were fragmented politically, there can be no doubt that the Hyksos were vital and energetic conquerors. After defeating the Egyptians in the Delta, one of their leaders, named Salitis or Saites, built a capital city at Avaris, somewhere along the easternmost branch of the Nile in the Delta. Saites took the title of pharaoh and founded the Fifteenth Dynasty. At approximately the same time, another group of Hyksos settled to the west of Avaris, in the center of the Delta, at a site called Sais, and founded the Fourteenth Dynasty. To confuse the picture even more, there is a Sixteenth Dynasty, made up of still other Hyksos, that was contemporary with the other two. We know nothing of relations between the three groups, nor why they were divided.

Below: This temple of Isis at Philae, begun during the reign of the Pharaoh Nectanebo I (380–362 B.C.), is important because it contains the last known inscription written in Egyptian hieroglyphics about A.D. 394. There is some informal graffiti on one of the walls that may be as late as A.D. 460. After that date, ancient hieroglyphics were a lost language until Jean-François Champollion learned how to read them again in A.D. 1822.

We do know something, however, about the relations of the Hyksos with the native Egyptian dynasty that ruled Upper Egypt to the south. The Hyksos were able to overcome the Egyptians in the Delta, but they were not able to subdue the Egyptian rulers whose capital was at Thebes. Somewhere south of Beni Hasan on the Nile, the Hyksos and the Egyptians established a frontier, and they ruled their respective parts of Egypt for nearly a century. Relations between the two groups were not necessarily warlike; in fact, there seem to have been long periods of peace. At times the two groups seem to have exchanged diplomatic missions, traded with one another, and even intermarried. Around 1580 Herit, a royal princess of Avaris and a daughter of the Hyksos pharaoh Apophis (c. 1585–1542), went south to marry a prince of Thebes.

The Hyksos' active foreign relations and trade were not limited to the Egyptians at Thebes. Hyksos artifacts, identified by the names of their rulers, have been found at Athens, Baghdad, Knossos, and Bogaskoy, so we know the Hyksos traded with the Mycenaean Greeks, the Kassites in Mesopotamia, Cretans, and Hittites in the area of modern Turkey. There are also records of diplomatic relations with the Nubian Kingdom south of the Second Cataract.

The Hyksos did not come to Egypt empty-handed. In fact, they were responsible for introducing into Egypt a number of items that would improve the country's economy. They developed a much more sophisticated method of making bronze that vastly improved the production of tools and weapons; they introduced the vertical loom, which increased the speed with which cloth could be made; and they brought in the pedal-

driven potter's wheel, which increased not only the amount of pottery a craftsman could make but also its quality. In addition, they brought olive and pomegranate trees, as well as the *zebu,* a type of hump-backed cattle.

The Hyksos, too, had a profound influence on the military heritage of Egypt. When they first entered Egypt as a military force, they came with scale armor, composite bows, bronze swords and daggers, and horses and chariots. If they did fight the Egyptians, they must have quickly defeated them, for the Egyptians at this time used only a simple bow and copper-tipped spears, and wore no armor at all. They went into battle wearing only kilts and carrying cowhide shields. It would seem that with this tremendous military advantage, the Hyksos could easily have taken the whole of Egypt, but for whatever reason—lack of unity or aggressiveness, perhaps—it seems they were content to allow the Egyptians to rule at Thebes.

The military superiority of the Hyksos was due to the chariot and the technology to turn it into an effective offensive weapon. The Hyksos chariot was extremely light—much of it was made out of wicker. It carried two men: a driver and a warrior, whose principal weapon was a composite bow made of laminated strips of bone and various kinds of hard wood. This weapon could shoot an arrow nearly 200 yards (183m), about three times the range of the standard Egyptian bow of the Twelfth Dynasty, which had an effective range of just over 70 yards (64m).

The tactic that evolved around the chariot was simple: a line of chariots approached an enemy forma-

tion at full gallop, wheeled to the right or left just out of range of the simple, unlamented or "self" bows of the enemy, and fired volley after volley at the enemy. It took skill and training to fire from a moving platform, but practice did make perfect, and between 1700 and 1100 this combined use of the chariot and composite bow was utilized by every army in the eastern Mediterranean basin. The Egyptians, who were not an inventive people but were certainly wise enough to imitate, rapidly adopted the superior weaponry of the Hyksos, and in time used it to drive the Hyksos out.

Hyksos vs. Thebans

Nobody has yet discovered the impetus for the hostilities that broke out between the Hyksos and the Thebans around 1560. The Hyksos were at that time ruled by one of their most gifted pharaohs, Apophis (1585–1542). In a New Kingdom source titled *The Quarrel of Apophis and Sekenenre,* it is written that

Above: In this particularly fine example of an Egyptian sarcophagus, hieroglyphics on the outside not only identify the occupant, but the inside surfaces might contain prayers and charms to protect the *ka,* or soul, on its journey to the judgment hall of Osiris.

Apophis provoked a quarrel with Sekenenre Tao II, the ruler of Thebes, by demanding that Sekenenre stop the bellowing of the hippopotamuses in the canal east of Thebes because they were preventing him from sleeping in his bedroom at Avaris. Since Thebes is over 350 miles (560km) south of Avaris, Sekenenre realized that Apophis' complaint was an excuse for war and launched an attack across the Hyksos-Egyptian frontier. Even though no evidence exists to substantiate this hypothesis, many historians believe that the Theban army must have been armed with the new composite bow and perhaps even chariots because attacking an enemy that had these weapons without having them yourself would be suicidal. Although the details of the attack are not known, it is known that Sekenenre died as a result of wounds received in battle.

Sekenenre's mummy was found in A.D. 1881 near the entrance to the Valley of the Kings, across the Nile from Luxor. When Sir Gaston Maspero unwrapped the pharaoh in 1886, he reported that the pharaoh had been struck in the jaw by a battle ax, then hit four more times on the top of the head. The skull revealed four jagged holes penetrating the bone. Maspero's autopsy revealed that the body of the king had started to decompose before mummification; this, combined with the fact that the king had been mummified at all, led Maspero to conclude that although the king had died on the field, his troops had recovered the body for burial. Fascinatingly, when the mummy of Sekenenre was X-rayed in 1986, the investigation revealed that some of the holes in the skull had begun to heal! Apparently, Sekenenre had survived the battle by some months, despite these grievous wounds and the inability of the Egyptian doctors to fight infection.

Bob Brier, an expert on Egyptian mummification, who in A.D. 1994 actually performed a mummification for the University of Maryland and the National Geographic Society, has speculated that the wounds were delivered while the king was lying down—perhaps asleep—because the angles of the blows are not consistent with those delivered to the head of a person standing upright. It is possible, therefore, that Sekenenre was assassinated in his sleep at Thebes while he was recovering from his battle wounds.

In any case, the battle against the Hyksos was renewed, with a vengeance, by Sekenenre's son Kamose, who ruled Upper Egypt from around 1555 to 1550. Either he or his brother Ahmose set up a stele at Karnak that describes how he planned to conquer the Hyksos, drink their wine, and enslave them to make still more wine. In this inscription he promised to destroy the trees in front of their temples, burn their towns, and cover the earth with their blood. And in an effort to fulfill this promise, Kamose launched a naval attack against the Hyksos about 50 miles (80km) south of the Fayum on the Nile.

Kamose captured their navy and moved on to Avaris. But Apophis shut himself up in Avaris and refused to come out. Kamose fumed at this cowardice, destroyed the farmland around the city, and insulted the wives of Apophis who every day gathered on the walls to watch the fighting. Kamose probably wondered why Apophis refused to fight, until his Egyptian scouts intercepted a message from Apophis to the King of Nubia. The letter revealed an alliance between the Hyksos and the Nubians, and detailed

a joint assault against the Egyptians in which the Hyksos would come from the north while the Nubians attacked from the south. Kamose called off his attack and retreated south toward Thebes.

Admiral Ahmose

Kamose, however, died at Thebes after a reign of only five years and was succeeded by his younger brother Ahmose. Because Ahmose was too young to lead armies at the time he succeeded, the war was put off for ten years. During this time, his mother, Ahhotep I, apparently ruled well as regent. She not only continued preparations for the resumption of hostilities, but foiled a coup against young Ahmose. By around 1545, Ahmose was ready to launch another attack against the Hyksos. Archaeologists are fortunate to have an unofficial source for this last campaign—a tomb inscription,

found at el-Kab in the tomb of an Egyptian admiral named Ahmose, about 35 miles (56km) south of Luxor, describes this official's rise through the ranks during the long war of liberation against the Hyksos.

This Ahmose, son of Ibana, records that he joined the new Egyptian army as a member of the crew of the warship *Wild Bull* when he was still a boy, or as he puts it, while he was still sleeping in a hammock (only a man who had his own house got to sleep in a real bed). Later, when he was an adult, he served aboard the warship *Northern*, which was used in the final campaign against Avaris. For a short time, it seems, he was ordered to fight on foot, as infantry, in support of the pharaoh's chariot corps. Soon after, however, he was assigned to a new ship named *Appearing at Memphis,* and was rewarded for valor in the battle to take the Pa-Djedku Canal outside the city of Avaris.

Apparently, the strategy was to capture the waterways surrounding Avaris, cut off supplies, and subject the city to siege. For a time, it seems the war devolved into a series of naval battles on the Nile and waterways around the city. Unfortunately, Admiral Ahmose does not supply details about the fall of the city, other than to say that during the campaign he fought hard and cut off the hands of several Hyksos as battle trophies. The pharaoh Ahmose was apparently pleased with this official's bravery and rewarded him not only with gold but with Egypt's highest military award, the Golden Fly—a small gold or silver replica of a fly that could be worn on a soldier's uniform.

Ahmose's account makes it clear that after the Egyptians drove the Hyksos out of Avaris, the latter retreated into Sharuhen, a Hyksos city in southern Israel, where Admiral Ahmose joined the pharaoh

Ahmose for an attack on that city. The admiral even helped to sack the town; he took more trophies of severed hands and won additional military honors for his efforts. He fought in two more battles for his pharaoh, this time in Nubia, after which he retired to live the life of a country gentlemen. He passed on his military heritage to his son, Ahmose Pennekheb, who left military memoirs on his own tomb recording his campaigns as a general in the army of Amenhotep I (1525–1505), the son of Pharaoh Ahmose. These memoirs are instructive because they chronicle how Egypt changed from a divided country fighting to free itself from foreign domination to an aggressive nation seeking to dominate other nations—all within the lifetimes of one man and his son.

THE NEW KINGDOM: THE CULTURE OF CONQUEST, 1550-1070

The New Kingdom begins with a new dynasty, the Eighteenth, which ruled Egypt for nearly 250 years and produced some of its greatest and most colorful rulers. We know much about these men and women because of the fortuitous discovery in A.D. 1881 of the remains of nearly forty pharaohs in a royal cache near the entrance to the famous Valley of the Kings.

The royal kings and queens in their coffins were packed together like sardines in one room roughly 17 feet (5m) square that was at the end of a 70-foot (21m) tunnel reached by a 40-foot (12m) shaft that had been dug straight down into solid rock. Many mummies of the great kings and queens of the Eighteenth Dynasty were there: Ahmose I; Tuthmosis II and III; Amenhotep I; Rameses I and II; Seti I; and an assortment of queens and royal priests.

One hundred feet (30m) farther back from this room was another room of similar size that contained the mummies of pharaohs and priests of the Twenty-first Dynasty (1070–945). It was the rulers of the Twenty-first Dynasty who discovered that many tombs in the Valley of the Kings had been robbed and subsequently removed the royal mummies to a remote spot. They were so sure that this tomb was a safe

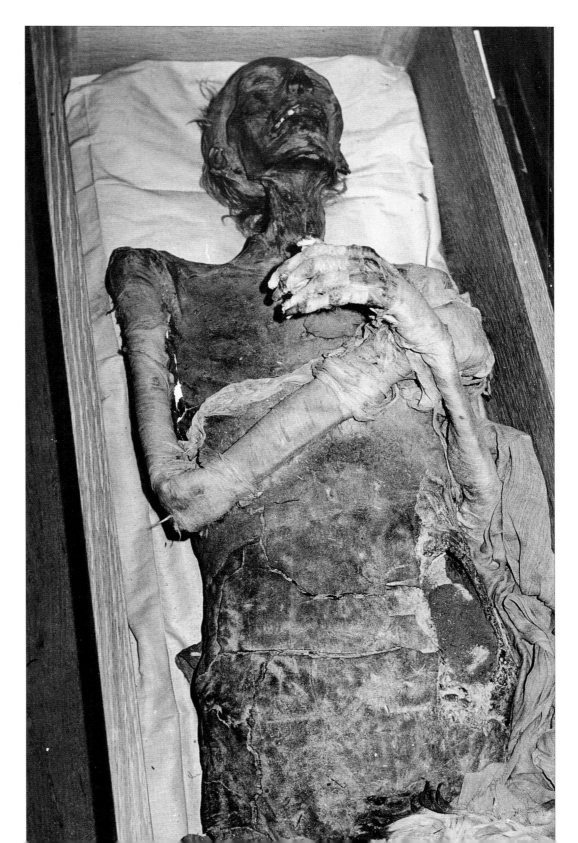

Below: The mummy of Rameses II, who ruled for sixty-six years, was first preserved by mummification and the dry Egyptian climate and later by modern scientific technology.

depository that they used it for their collective tomb; their certainty seems to have been reasonable, for the tomb with its royal occupants lay undiscovered for three thousand years.

Around A.D. 1870, however, an enterprising family of local tomb robbers, led by the Abd er Rassul family, discovered the cache and began harvesting it to supply the lucrative antiquities market. The money was distributed among the inhabitants of the village of Goornah, who had been made poor by incredibly high taxes. This source of income ceased when Gaston Maspero, director of the Egyptian Antiquities Service, discovered the tomb in A.D. 1881 and removed all the mummies to the Cairo Museum.

Seventeen years later, in 1898, Victor Loret, the new director of the Egyptian Antiquities Service, discovered another cache of New Kingdom mummies.

In the tomb of Amenhotep II (1427–1401) Loret discovered the mummies of Tuthmosis IV; Amenhotep III; Merneptah; Siptah; Rameses IV, V, and VI; Queen Tye, the wife of Amenhotep II; a son of Amenhotep II, Webensennu; plus two as yet unidentified mummies. The mummies of Queen Tye, Amenhotep II, and Webensennu had been badly mutilated in antiquity when tomb robbers tore open their chests in search of the heart scarab, a heavily jeweled artifact that the New Kingdom embalmers placed in the heart cavity of a mummy.

The discovery of these two royal caches made it possible for the first time to study the remains of the historical personages of the New Kingdom. Most recently, scientists have begun to subject these royal mummies to DNA analysis, a process that holds promise for the future as a way to explain a great deal about the previously obscure genealogy of the New Kingdom royal line.

The mummies in these caches have helped make the New Kingdom the most familiar era of Egyptian history for the modern layman. There is, after all, a certain ghoulish fascination with these dead bodies and the dark tombs in which they lay. But even if the mummies had not been discovered, the New Kingdom would be a relatively familiar subject because enough of the art, architecture, literature, and sculpture from this period has survived to give us a detailed and intimate portrait of the men and women who ruled Egypt at this time. Furthermore, their accomplishments in the field of building and military conquest are truly monumental and have lasted centuries.

something at Karnak, and it rapidly became the showplace of Egypt.

Karnak, however, is its modern name. In ancient times the Egyptians called it Petisut, or The Most Holy of Places. This site is a vast area covering nearly one square mile, which makes it the largest single religious site in the world. The main complex was called the Precinct of Amun and was, as its name suggests, dedicated to this god. The New Kingdom pharaohs made a point of putting the god Amun (also Amon or Amen, in some sources) at the center of their religious building program. Amun was originally an Upper Egyptian deity, and by stressing his importance in their kingdom, the New Kingdom pharaohs were making a conscious effort to "demote" Re, who had been associated with Lower Egypt, where the hated Hyksos embraced Re and even invoked him in their official titles. From the time of their ascendancy, the New Kingdom pharaohs placed the name Re after that of Amun so that Amun, the Theban manifestation of the sun god, was definitely superior to Re, the Memphis deity.

The Precinct of Amun at Karnak is dominated by a great temple that has two main parts, one running east-west, the other north-south. No matter how one approaches the temple, the entrance to the sanctuary is through ten massive rectangular, truncated stone pyramids known as pylons, some of which are 79 feet (24m) high. In archeology, the pylons are listed and identified by number as pylons I–X. Today, the outward-facing fronts of these pylons are covered with stone reliefs, but during the New Kingdom those reliefs were covered with thin beaten gold sheets that accented the reliefs and recorded for posterity the exploits of which-

The Great Temple at Karnak

It was the pharaohs of the New Kingdom who began a totally new and active tradition of building temples throughout Egypt out of stone. During the Old Kingdom, pharaohs had built stone temples, but only as part of their tomb complexes. In the Middle Kingdom, the pharaohs built numerous temples within the major cities of Egypt, but these temples were made of mud brick that did not survive the centuries. The most important and impressive temple site of the New Kingdom is Karnak, which was built less than a mile north of the New Kingdom capital of Thebes. Every pharaoh of the New Kingdom felt impelled to build

Khons, Ptah, and Osiris, and others to the pharaohs Amenhotep II, Rameses III, and Tuthmosis III. The most impressive of these temples is that of Tuthmosis III (1479–1425), which lies directly behind the main sanctuary. Part of it is called the Botanical Garden, because its walls are covered with plants, animals, and exotic birds. Temples to Mut, Rameses III, and the vizier Khonsepehkhrod, plus a lake, also lie within the walls of this precinct.

To the south of the Precinct of Amun lies the Precinct of Mut, the vulture-headed goddess wife of Amun-Re who was one of the original deities of Thebes. Within the walls of this precinct there was once a lake. Finally, just north of the Precinct of Amun is the Precinct of Month, the war god of Upper Egypt. This god usually appears as a man with the head of a hawk; a solar disk and two plumes frame his head, and he is generally pictured carrying a scimitar, a saber with a curved blade.

Each succeeding pharaoh felt the need to outdo the one before him in building at Karnak. By about the middle of the New Kingdom, Karnak and the numerous other temples the pharaohs supported

ever pharaoh built the pyramid upon which they were carved. Behind the pylons at Karnak is the sacred temple of Amun-Re, in which the priests made their daily rituals and performed ritual sacrifices.

Twenty smaller temples also stand within the Precinct of Amun, including ones to the gods Opet,

had grown to become an economic force in themselves that controlled one third the revenue of Egypt and gave employment to 20 percent of the population. One hundred twenty-five years after the founding of the Eighteenth Dynasty, the priesthood of Amun had become so powerful that Amenhotep II felt that the priests' power threatened his own, and he tried to bring their power under control by appointing only members of his family to the various high priesthoods. Tuthmosis IV (1401–1391) and Amenhotep III (1391–1353) continued this practice during their reigns, and Amenhotep even revived the cult of Re as a theological counterweight to the priests of Amun.

Amenhotep I (1525–1505), the son of Ahmose, was the only New Kingdom pharaoh who did not have time to do much building, for he was burdened with the task of creating a political framework on which to hang the new empire that his father had left him. He did, however, make one far-reaching contribution to the architectural heritage of Egypt by deciding not to build a pyramid to house his remains. Instead, he was the first pharaoh to be buried in a rock cut-tomb, a tomb cut into standing rock, such as a cliff face. The tomb, near the village of Dira Abu'n Naga near Thebes, was not only hidden but separated from his funerary temple where the priests performed the burial

rites. The reason behind this innovation was probably nothing more than that he wanted his tomb and its rich furnishings hidden from tomb robbers.

Amenhotep I may have been too busy establishing a firm political framework to build extensively, but he was the only pharaoh of the Eighteenth Dynasty of whom this was true. Tuthmosis I (1504–1492), the son of Amenhotep I and a nonroyal wife, succeeded his father to the throne and married his half-sister to strengthen his claim to the throne. He became the founder of the Egyptian empire whose borders stretched from the Euphrates to Nubia, and he used the wealth gained from these conquests to become one of Egypt's great builders.

It was Tuthmosis who began the monumental building campaign at Karnak. He completely rebuilt the Temple of Amun, which his forefathers had erected, enclosing it behind a high stone wall. He then enhanced the prestige of the temple architecturally by building two massive pylons at the front of the temple with a large entry hall in between. This hall had fourteen pillars that were representations of the papyrus plant. At the time they were built, Tuthmosis had them covered with gold to make an even greater impression. In front of his first pylon he erected two obelisks. The temple that he built at Karnak became a prototype for all other temples built in the New Kingdom.

THE SECOND INTERMEDIATE PERIOD AND
THE NEW KINGDOM

Right: A painting from the Nineteenth Dynasty shows a carpenter working with an adze. The painting is unique among Egyptian representations of workmen, since the worker is unshaven and has disheveled hair. **Opposite:** Rameses II raises his hands in supplication to the god Horus in a relief from Amun's Temple at Luxor. Horus is always shown with a hawk's head.

Tuthmosis' Tomb

Across the Nile from Thebes, in the great desert defile that came to be called the Valley of the Kings, Tuthmosis built a concealed tomb like that of his father. He was the first pharaoh to build a tomb at this famous site (his father's tomb was built somewhat to the north of Thebes), which lies behind a screen of high cliffs that block the valley from the Nile River Valley. The Valley of the Kings is the head of a great wadi formed hundreds of thousands of years ago when it was the main channel of a river that flowed into the Nile. At the time, Egypt had been green and fertile, home to elephants, antelope, and other beasts that are now found a thousand miles (1600km) south of Egypt in Kenya and Tanzania. The Valley also supported a large population of wandering hunters who left behind piles of flint flakes struck from their primitive tools.

Tuthmosis' architect, Ineni, who had supervised the king's construction at Karnak, also supervised his tomb's construction in this great dry valley. A long inscription on the walls of Ineni's tomb discusses how he had the tomb built secretly and allowed no one to see it. The workmen and artisans used for this construction lived in a special village built by Tuthmosis at

Deir el Medina, near the mouth of the Valley of the Kings, to serve as home to a permanent party of skilled workers and artists whose sole function was to build, maintain, and protect the royal tombs in the valley.

The town of Deir el Medina was continuously inhabited for the next 450 years, and supplied not only workers to build the tombs by day but also a large number of people—in many cases, probably the same people—to rob the tombs by night. A papyrus from the year 1117 B.C. records the official investigation of a series of tomb robberies that took place in that year. The document summarizes the investigation, questioning, and trial of the culprits. A subsequent house-to-house search in Deir el Medina resulted in the recovery of many of the stolen items. In this case, the guilty people were not the workmen who built the tombs but a group of temple attendants whose job it was to maintain the various funerary temples in the Valley.

Tuthmosis' tomb, the first one built in the Valley of the Kings, has been found; in fact, two tombs that once housed Tuthmosis have been discovered. The first was the tomb he probably had built for himself, and the second was one built by his daughter, Hatshepsut, as a final resting place for both herself and her father. Tuthmosis I's mummy was not found in

Right: The god Anubis offers the *ankh*, the symbol of life, to Tuthmosis II. **Below:** The Egyptians prized family life, and statues of husbands with their wives seated beside them are common. This one is from an Eighteenth Dynasty tomb at Saqqara. **Opposite:** The northern portal of the temple complex at Karnak leads from the Precinct of Amun to the Precinct of Montu.

either tomb. It may have been moved for safekeeping by the pharaohs of the Twenty-first Dynasty to the so-called royal cache, but we cannot be sure. The embalmers of the Twenty-first Dynasty had rewrapped Tuthmosis, but Psusennes I of that dynasty had stolen Tuthmosis' coffin for his own use. Egyptologists found a mummy which they thought was Tuthmosis stacked in the first room of the cache at Deir el Bahri with several other royal mummies. This mummy was so identified because he bore a striking resemblance to the mummies of Tuthmosis II and III, whose remains were in the same burial chamber.

In A.D. 1980, however, the University of Chicago published *An X-ray Atlas of the Royal Mummies*, and that source revealed that the mummy traditionally identified as Tuthmosis I was in reality a twenty-two-year-old man. No record survives to indicate how old Tuthmosis was when he died, but had he died at twenty-two he would have had to have been a boy of around six when he ascended the throne. No evidence indicates that he ruled as a boy king, so it seems likely that Tuthmosis has not been found. What, then, happened to him?

Perhaps he is buried somewhere awaiting discovery. It is equally likely, however, that his was one of the numerous unidentified mummies carted off between the end of the eighteenth and the beginning of the twentieth century A.D. for ghoulish

exhibitions called "unwrappings," in which Egyptologists and charlatans alike participated and which were attended by capacity crowds. Mummies were also bought for souvenirs. In A.D. 1874 Amelia Edwards, an English writer who was cruising on the Nile near the Valley of the Kings, bought a mummy from the Abd er Rassul family, the same family that had been harvesting the royal cache for several years. Unfortunately, a few days after the buy, the mummy began to smell, and Ms. Edwards had it thrown overboard into the Nile. Could it have been Tuthmosis I?

Hatshepsut

Upon his death, Tuthmosis I was succeeded by his son Tuthmosis II (1492–1479). To secure the succession and ensure that no one could question his legitimacy, Tuthmosis II married his half-sister, the renowned Hatshepsut, who was Tuthmosis I's daughter by his chief wife. We know little about Tuthmosis II's reign. Some evidence indicates that he might have campaigned against the Nubians, but it is equally possible that these campaigns were those of his son Tuthmosis III. He left only a small funerary temple, and his tomb has never been identified. He may have been buried in

The goddess Isis, transformed into a sycamore tree, breast-feeds the very young pharaoh Tuthmosis III. The larger figure standing behind the suckling pharaoh is Tuthmosis III as an adult, holding the mace symbolizing power. The picture may be propaganda claiming that Tuthmosis III is descended directly from Isis, and therefore has a good claim to the throne. **Below:** Part of a foundation stone from a temple at Karnak cites Hatshepsut and her dedication of the temple to the god Amun.

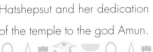

his father's tomb after Hatshepsut had moved Tuthmosis I to her tomb.

Hatshepsut certainly overshadowed Tuthmosis II. She outlived her brother-husband, and consequently succeeded him and ruled as pharaoh in her own right from 1473 to 1458. Hatshepsut has fascinated students of Egypt for centuries.

When Tuthmosis II died, Tuthmosis III, his ten-year-old son by a palace slave named Isis, was considered too young to rule alone.

Tuthmosis III was duly crowned pharaoh and married to his aunt Hatshepsut, with the understanding that she would serve as regent until he became an adult. In a sense, Hatshepsut had a better blood claim to the throne than Tuthmosis III, for she had no common blood in her veins, being the daughter of Tuthmosis I and his sister-wife Ahmose, who was herself the younger sister of Amenhotep I. Yet strong as her claim may have been, the tradition had always been that a male heir had a better claim to the throne than a female one.

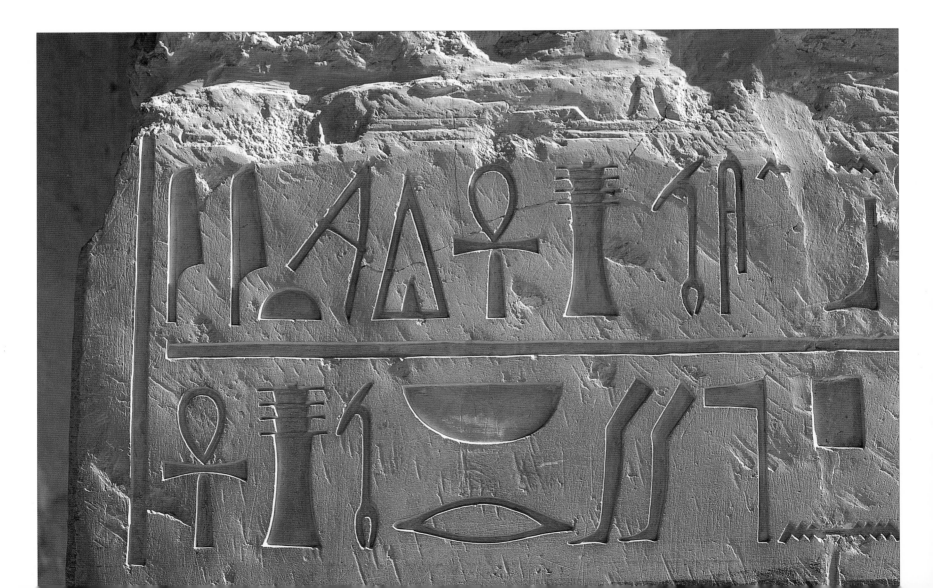

This powerful woman would not, however, be overshadowed for long. In the first year of her reign, Hatshepsut gathered around her a group of male advisors, many of whom had served her father. In the second year of her joint reign, she assumed control of the government, declared herself pharaoh, and thrust Tuthmosis III into a subservient role. After claiming the office, she went on to cement her position by representing herself as a man. On official occasions, she even wore the long, narrow beard of a pharaoh and had her sculptors cut monuments that used the pronouns he and his in referring to events of her reign.

If this masculinization of her seems ridiculous, a great deal of her other propaganda efforts were not. The details of them were cut into the walls of her mortuary temple at Deir el Bahri. According to the inscription, Hatshepsut was not the daughter of Tuthmosis I at all, but of the great god Amun who had visited her mother one night in the royal palace. In a scene reminiscent of the Greek god Zeus' seduction of Hercules' mother, Alcmene, wherein the god changed himself into the image of the lady's husband, Amun changed himself into the image of Amenhotep—thus preserving Ahmose's honor. The seduction scene is spelled out in some detail, to the extent that when the very proper Victorian archaeologist James Henry Breasted translated the inscription in his *Ancient Records of Egypt* (published in A.D. 1906), he felt impelled to render the description of the god's erection and the queen's reaction to it in Latin instead of English so it would neither offend nor arouse the uneducated.

The god Khnum, the heavenly potter who makes souls, fashioned a royal *ka* for the infant Hatshepsut. The child, therefore, was semidivine, and when she was crowned became more divine than human. The god Thoth, who presided over magic

and who invented writing, appears in the Deir el Bahri reliefs as a heavenly messenger sent to tell Ahmose about the coming glory of the child she would bear. The whole scene was intended to underline the legitimacy of Hatshepsut's assumption of power.

From the records that remain, we know that Hatshepsut's propaganda worked, and that she was accepted wholeheartedly by the political powers of Egypt. She appears to have ruled over a prosperous nation and to have advertised that prosperity through her building projects. Her most famous creation is the mortuary temple at Deir el Bahri, which she named Djeser-Djeseru, or The Holy of Holies. In many ways this structure is reminiscent of the mortuary temple of Mentuhotep, the great pharaoh of the Eleventh Dynasty, that sits next to Hatshepsut's temple. It is certain that Senemut, Hatshepsut's architect, received the inspiration for Djeser-Djeseru from Mentuhotep's earlier temple complex, for both have distinct terraces that sit

Below: Hatshepsut offers a jar to a god. She wears a false beard, the standard symbol for a pharaoh, which she wore on ceremonial occasions.

against the same high desert cliff, and both are connected by wide ramps that ascend from the Nile. Yet Hatshepsut's design is larger and more grand.

Hatshepsut's Temple

In the topmost section of Hatshepsut's temple a funerary sanctuary is situated wherein the priests would perform the ceremonies preparing her *ka* for its difficult journey to the realm of Osiris. Yet the most imposing section of the temple is the area of reliefs that cover the inside walls of the pillared porticoes of the middle and lower colonnades. One of those reliefs is the account of her mother's miraculous impregnation by the god Amun; another records the transport of the two great obelisks from Aswan to Thebes. These are

justly famous, but both are overshadowed by the celebrated depiction of the voyage to Punt.

To a New Kingdom Egyptian, Punt represented the farthest imaginable destination from Egypt. If it lay, as archaeologists suspect, on the coast of Eretria or Somalia, the only way to reach it was via a long voyage down the Red Sea. Built without keels and held together by a rope that ran the length of the ship, Egyptian vessels were strong enough to navigate the Nile, but an extended voyage, even on a relatively tideless body of water like the Red Sea, was quite another matter. The risks were worth the effort, however, because Punt was the source of luxury goods that fed the funerary culture of ancient Egypt. The royal house needed myrrh, frankincense, and incense for their elaborate funereal ceremonies, and ebony, gold, and ivory

for the luxury furniture and coffin decorations. Punt was also the best place to find pygmies, which were still immensely popular in New Kingdom Egypt.

The reliefs at Deir el Bahri detail the voyage of five ships, loaded with soldiers and trade goods, down the Red Sea to the coast of Punt. Upon arrival, the leader of the expedition, Hatshepsut's favored advisor, Neshi (the Egyptian word for "black man" or "Nubian"), goes ashore in a small boat loaded with trade goods consisting of necklaces, weapons, beads, axes, and daggers. Neshi is shown being greeted by the ruler of the Puntians, Pe-re-hu, and his grossly overweight wife, Ety. The illustrations go on to picture the

Egyptian crew loading complete myrrh trees aboard their ships, along with a collection of live monkeys, bags of gold, elephant tusks, and panther skins. The reliefs do not include a representation of the return voyage, but the final scene is of the treasures being unloaded in Thebes before the eyes of Hatshepsut.

How the ships got from Thebes to the coast of the Red Sea, and then back again after the voyage, is a matter of some debate. A few scholars have suggested that a canal between the Nile and the northernmost arm of the Red Sea via the Bitter Lake or Lake Timsah must have been the way, but most believe that the ships were built to be taken apart, carried overland to the port of Quseir, reassembled, and then launched.

Whatever the route of the expedition, its successful completion would have been a decided success for Hatshepsut.

The great temple at Djeser-Djeseru was not built to serve only as a mortuary temple for the queen; it had an important function as well in the calendar of religious events that determined life in Egypt. Every summer the Egyptians held an event dedicated to the god Amun; this was called the Feast of the Valley. For most of the year, Amun's great statue was housed in his temple at Karnak. For the feast, it was taken from Karnak, drawn to the banks of the Nile, placed on a barge, and floated to Djeser-Djeseru, where willing hands hauled it up the

assumption of the throne, and she was willing to amend the truth when the occasion improved her position.

In her building at Karnak, Hatshepsut also did not neglect to build a temple to Amun, the god who was so important to her legitimacy. Within this temple, she built the famous Red Chapel, a structure cut from red quartzite that was built to hold the barge on which the Amun statue rode during the Feast of the Valley on its journey from Karnak to Djeser-Djeseru.

Senemut

Certainly one of the most fascinating aspects of Hatshepsut's reign, and one that has fascinated students of Egypt for centuries, was the queen's relationship with her most trusted advisor, Senemut. This relationship is all the more mysterious because in an age when only nobles advised the pharaoh, Senemut, easily the most powerful man in her administration, was a commoner. Throughout his lifetime, he held the title of Chief Overseer of the King's Works (Hatshepsut often referred to herself as a king), Steward of the Wealth of Amun, Royal Tutor to the Princess Neferure (Hatshepsut's daughter by Tuthmosis II), and Overseer of the Works of Amun, to name only a few out of probably two dozen appellations. Evidence of his power is everywhere — over

ramps to a special sanctuary where it would be joined with Hathor so the priests could perform sacred rites. By building Djeser-Djeseru, Hatshepsut joined in this age-old ritual and associated herself with the god Amun. What better way to prove her tie to her heavenly father?

The great temple complex at Deir el Bahri, with its magnificent design, marvelous reliefs, graphic graffiti, and mysterious tomb for a commoner, was not the only architectural monument to Hatshepsut. She also built a temple to the lion-headed goddess Sekhmet near Beni Hasan, in which she reaffirmed her relationship with her father Amun, and she commissioned inscriptions that lauded herself as the savior of Egypt who had ended the chaos of the Hyksos menace. This was a bit of an exaggeration, since her grandfather, Ahmose, had been the one who had driven the enemy from Egypt, but Hatshepsut was anxious to justify her sixty inscriptions and statues of him exist throughout the queen's temple at Deir el Bahri. Perhaps even more amazing is that he apparently built a tomb for himself beneath Hatshepsut's great temple. The fact that he was allowed to do this, an act unthinkable for anyone outside the royal family, certainly indicates some kind of relationship between the two other than that of a trusted advisor to his ruler.

Historians have, of course, speculated about Senemut's relationship to Hatshepsut. Earlier in this century, when the attitude toward women was decidedly biased against their ability, Senemut was portrayed as the secret manipulator of Hatshepsut. Her will was not regarded as her own, and this clever and ruthless man was thought to have planned and controlled her ascent to power. More recently, he has been seen as a gifted

earthly father, Tuthmosis I, who had instructed her to do so in order to praise her heavenly father, Amun. The upper part of both obelisks were covered in gold leaf, which would have been especially impressive sparkling in the bright Egyptian sun.

The Death of Hatshepsut

We know very little about the death of Hatshepsut. Romantic imagination has created a legend that Tuthmosis III, her nephew/husband/stepson, murdered her because his marriage to Hatshepsut had been imposed and because he had suffered her disdain while she conducted the affair with her lover, Senemut. According to this story, after he murdered her, Tuthmosis went on a rampage of destruction, cutting her name from her many monuments in an attempt to erase her memory and perhaps to take revenge; obliterating her name would cause her a second death in the afterlife, for it was believed that the *ka* survived only as long as some remnant of the deceased—be it the mummy, portrait, or name—survived. There is, however, no absolutely concrete evidence upon which to base these musings.

administrator who simply advised Hatshepsut, who in turn saw his abilities and promoted him accordingly.

The question remains, did a romantic relationship exist between the two? We will probably never know, but a number of graffiti inscriptions in the vicinity of Deir el Bahri, probably scratched into the rock by workers, allude to an illicit affair between Senemut and Hatshepsut. One particularly graphic example has a female figure wearing the royal crown bent over while a male figure in a workman's cap enters her from the rear. Does this kind of representation have any validity? Such a crude scrawl is perhaps nothing more than some ancient Egyptian man's discomfort with the existence of a powerful woman.

Just outside the Fifth Pylon at Karnak, which stood in front of the Red Chapel, Hatshepsut erected two obelisks, both measuring nearly 97 feet (30m) tall. Obelisks symbolized the rays of the sun and were a unique Egyptian contribution to architecture. To erect the two obelisks outside the Red Chapel, Hatshepsut had to tear down part of the hypostyle temple that her father had built. However, she was careful to state that she did this only at the express wish of her departed

What evidence we do have reflects much more credit on both Hatshepsut and Tuthmosis III. We know that Tuthmosis was never consigned to the royal "scrap heap" during Hatshepsut's reign. In fact, during her lifetime he led campaigns into Nubia. From youth, he had been trained as a soldier, a role in which he apparently flourished. Records survive of Tuthmosis leading no less than fourteen major military expeditions into the area that today comprises Israel, Lebanon, and southern Syria. There are also records of Tuthmosis leading expeditions into Nubia. There is evidence that Hatshepsut accompanied him on at least one of these journeys. Monuments to Tuthmosis reveal that he was especially skilled as an archer and gave public exhibitions of his ability to shoot arrows accurately at targets while riding in a chariot being drawn at full gallop. He was undoubtedly a first-class military man with strong ties to the regular Egyptian army.

Did he resent being made subservient to a powerful woman? Probably, but when he became pharaoh he was only ten, and by the time he was old enough to oppose her, Hatshepsut was already too firmly established for him to have any hope of shaking her from the throne. Besides, by that time Hatshepsut was probably in her mid-forties, and Tuthmosis knew that he only had to wait for her death (at this time people were considered old if they lived into their fifties) to ascend peacefully to the throne. In any case, she must have trusted him, for he certainly could have used army connections to initiate a coup d'etat.

If the evidence is considered, the idea that Tuthmosis III immediately set about to erase Hatshepsut's memory when he became pharaoh in 1458 simply does not hold up. Judging by the discovery of pieces of her wooden coffin at the site where the priests of the Twenty-first Dynasty rewrapped and restored the royal mummies before they reburied them in the royal cache, he apparently gave her an honorable burial. And though Hatshepsut's mummy has not been found, the coffin fragments lead us to believe that there was a mummy of Hatshepsut surviving for at least five hundred years after her death. We also know that many of her inscriptions survived the reign of Tuthmosis III and were obscured only by the building projects of later pharaohs.

What does seem to be true is that in the very last years of his reign, Tuthmosis decided on a deliberate policy to destroy some of the titles of Hatshepsut—those that

THE SECOND INTERMEDIATE PERIOD AND
THE NEW KINGDOM

named her as a ruling pharaoh. However, he left the inscriptions that name her as the queen consort. His motive in this selective destruction was probably simple. He realized that after he was dead, some might choose to challenge his legitimacy on the basis of his predecessor's decision to defy propriety and rule as a man. Perhaps he feared that the conservative Egyptians might want to disqualify from the rank of pharaoh anyone who had contributed to this bizarre anomaly. This reasoned, pragmatic approach seems to

have been entirely consistent with what we know of Tuthmosis III, and he very nearly succeeded in his efforts to redefine Hatshepsut's role in history. Various lists of rulers chiseled in stone at Abydos and Saqqara omit her name from the roster of New Kingdom pharaohs. If it had not been for the historian Manetho, who recorded a female pharaoh between Tuthmosis II and III, archaeologists might never have suspected her existence, and so might have neglected to search for her amid the ruins they excavated.

Below: The Table of Abydos from the Temple of Rameses II at Abydos is one of the most important sources for the chronology of the early pharaohs of Egypt because it lists sixty-six pharaohs from the earliest times to Rameses himself, with the notable exception of Hatshepsut.

THE SECOND INTERMEDIATE PERIOD AND
THE NEW KINGDOM

Right: In addition being worn daily, tunics and loincloths were often buried in tombs so the dead would have something to wear in the afterlife. **Below:** The Blue Crown of Egypt features the traditional color of the kings of the Eighteenth Dynasty and of Upper Egypt. **Opposite:** Although the Egyptians used obelisks, such as this one of Tuthmosis I, to record the glorious deeds of their pharaohs, the word obelisk comes from a Greek obscenity. Greek mercenary soldiers serving in Egypt from the seventh century B.C. on labeled these monuments, and the word has unfortunately stuck.

Tuthmosis III

Because of his military conquests, building activities, and literary accomplishments, Tuthmosis III stands out as the greatest of all the rulers of ancient Egypt. He was a prodigious builder, and he used the tremendous wealth that his sixteen military campaigns brought home from Palestine and Syria to finance it all.

He expanded, beautified, and completely restored the great Temple of Amun at Karnak. He also added a pylon and two obelisks in front of the central court and sanctuary to Amun, and constructed a magnificent festival court behind the central court. The walls of the festival court were originally covered with painted stone reliefs of exotic animals and plants that he either saw or brought home from Syria. Prominent among these animals are elephants, which Tuthmosis hunted in that country near the banks of the Euphrates River. The reliefs at Karnak do not mention it, but the tomb inscriptions of a courtier named Amenemhab describe how the pharaoh was nearly killed by an elephant. During one elephant hunt, the beast turned on Tuthmosis and caught him in the middle of a river, nearly trampling him to death. Amenemhab saved the pharaoh's life by distracting the animal: he interposed himself between Tuthmosis and the elephant and sliced off the tip of the animal's trunk (which the courtier called a hand), which resulted in the elephant chasing Amenemhab instead. The brave courtier wedged himself between two great rocks where the elephant could not get at him. The story must have an element of truth in it, for after they returned from Syria, Amenemhab was richly rewarded with gold and clothing and was promoted to high command in the army.

Other reliefs at Karnak preserve legends about Tuthmosis III that reinforce his divinity and close relations with the god Amun. As a junior priest in Amun's temple, Tuthmosis stood in the background during the Feast of the Valley, while the shrine of Amun was carried around the temple. In the middle of the ceremony, the shrine began to mysteriously move among the throng, and it stopped in front of Tuthmosis. The boy threw himself to the ground, but the god emerged from the shrine, raised him to his feet, and changed him into a falcon. The two then flew away to heaven, where Amun crowned Tuthmosis pharaoh. The story served to reinforce the pharaoh's claim to the throne.

Tuthmosis III ordered the erection of monuments and temples all over Egypt. At Kom Medinet Ghurab, a mile and a half (2.4km) southwest of Lahun, he built a temple to Amun. He built similar temples at

Semna, below the Second Cataract; one at el-Lessiya, north of Abu Simbel; and one at Heliopolis, just north of modern Cairo. However, the most famous of his monuments—the obelisks—are not in Egypt at all, for they were moved by people who came long after the time of Tuthmosis, to sites in Rome, Istanbul, London, and New York City. Arguably the most well known of these stands in New York's Central Park. For decades, this obelisk has been called Cleopatra's Needle by a public for whom that famous queen is synonymous with ancient Egypt. One can only imagine how Tuthmosis, with a childhood spent in the shadow of another powerful Egyptian queen, would react.

Tuthmosis' engineers cut this obelisk and its mate, which now adorns the Embankment on the Thames River in London, from quarries of red granite near Aswan in southern Egypt, and floated them down the Nile to Heliopolis. Both are 70 feet (21m) high and weigh 225 tons. In the year 12 B.C., the Roman emperor Augustus (27 B.C.–A.D. 14) moved them from Heliopolis to Alexandria, where they remained until A.D. 1869, when the Egyptian government made gifts of them to the governments of the United States and Great Britain.

It took twelve years, however, for the U.S. government to figure out how to get the monstrous piece of stone to Central Park. William Vanderbilt, a millionaire philanthropist from New York, volunteered to pay for the obelisk's transportation and persuaded the U.S. Navy to handle the operation. Vanderbilt bought an Egyptian steamer and had it modified to receive the great monolith through the deck, which allowed the obelisk to lie safely in the hold. When owners of the various dry docks in New York City set outrageous sums for the use of their facilities, Vanderbilt had the obelisk unloaded on Staten Island,

where it was attached to pontoons and drawn by tug boats to West 96th Street. From there it was carried via a temporary railroad, built on giant wooden beams that spared the street, through Central Park to East 86th Street, then down Fifth Avenue to its final site, near East 81st Street. It had taken the U.S. Navy thirty-eight days to ferry Tuthmosis' "Needle" across the Atlantic, but it took Vanderbilt's men 112 days to get it from Staten Island to Central Park.

Tuthmosis was succeeded by his son Amenhotep II (1427–1401), who was in turn succeeded by his son Tuthmosis IV (1400–1392). Neither was especially noted for his building programs. But Tuthmosis IV's son, Amenhotep III (1391–1353), is justly called The Magnificent because of his extensive construction projects at Karnak and Luxor.

The Temples of Amenhotep III

Amenhotep III's greatest architectural effort was at Luxor, a mile and a half from Karnak. There he rebuilt and greatly expanded a temple to Amun. This temple figured prominently in the yearly ceremony during which the statue of Amun was brought from Karnak to Luxor. Amun, accompanied by his wife, Khons, and son Mut, were pulled by priests to the Nile, loaded on boats, and rowed down the river accompanied by trumpet choruses, chanting, and dancing. Surprisingly, the ceremonial procession is still repeated every year, though in modified form. Today, Amun has given way to a Moslem saint named Abu Haggag, whose small boat the Moslem faithful carry through the streets of modern Thebes all the way from his mosque built on a small part of the Luxor temple. While the procession no longer goes to the Amun Temple at Karnak, it is too similar to the old Egyptian ceremony to be anything

but a reenactment of a custom that these modern people's ancestors carried out 3,400 years ago.

The temple that Amenhotep built for the god's "visit" has been justly celebrated as the epitome of ancient Egyptian architecture. It is unique because it is almost completely the work of Amenhotep and has not been adulterated by additions from other pharaohs. About a century later, Rameses II built his own temple to Amun, which is attached to the front of Amenhotep's, but its being there does not detract from the aesthetics and integrity of the building. In its basic outline, the temple at Luxor was like most Egyptian temples, but its details and grand proportions make it special.

The temple complex begins with a colonnaded hall dominated by fourteen giant columns in the shape of stylized papyrus plants set in two rows and running down the center. These middle columns are much higher than the colonnade walls on either side, so that the roof of the hall admits light through a clerestory. Proceeding through this hall, one comes to a forecourt with sixty-four columns in the shape of unopened papyrus plants surrounding an open courtyard. The walls that enclose the columns and the courtyard are covered with reliefs depicting the great events of Amenhotep's reign. In ancient times, these carvings were painted over for added drama.

The south end of this forecourt consists of a hypostyle hall that leads through a smaller court to the so-called birth room, the walls of which are covered with drawings showing the sacred birth of the pharaoh. Reminiscent of the birth images commissioned by Hatshepsut, these scenes picture the king's mother, Mutemweya, the daughter of King Artatama I of Mitanni, with the god Amun disguised as Amenhotep's father, Tuthmosis IV. An accompanying relief panel shows the goddesses Isis and Khnum leading Mutemweya into a birthing room.

About a mile and a half north of Luxor is the temple complex at Karnak that holds so many remnants of the construction of the New Kingdom pharaohs. Amenhotep III's most famous contribution at Karnak was a great pylon (number III) that stands today between a pylon of Tuthmosis I (number IV) and the great hypostyle hall of Rameses II. This 79-foot (24m) pylon bears reliefs that summarize some of the major events of Amenhotep's reign. In ancient times, these reliefs were accented with two substances: thin sheets of beaten gold hammered into the stone cuttings, and a half-ton of malachite set in grooves and holes cut into the images. On either side of the entryway through the pylon were two lapis

Directly across from Karnak lay the pharaoh's great mortuary temple. We can only guess at its size, for it has completely disappeared except for two huge statues of the seated king that at one time stood on either side of its entrance. Although hieroglyphs clearly identify these two giant statues as depictions of Amenhotep III, the ancient world quickly forgot this and assumed that the northern statue was a representation of Memnon, the mythical son of the goddess of dawn, Aurora, and her human lover Tithonus, prince of Troy. In antiquity, this statue achieved some notoriety, for each day at dawn, as the rising sun warmed the statue, it gave off a low humming sound. Legend held that this was the sound of Memnon singing to his mother. Unfortunately, the statue suffered the same fate as the Sphinx—it served as a target for Turkish artillery practice—and it no longer gives off this strange sound.

Above: The royal colonnade hall of Amenhotep III at the Temple of Amun at Luxor is flanked by two seated statues of Rameses II. Although Amenhotep III had built the hall almost a century before Rameses ruled, Rameses saw nothing wrong with adding his own statues to it.

lazuli stelae. The effect of all this gold and brightly polished stone glimmering in the sun must have been overwhelming.

South of this great temple complex, Amenhotep III built a temple to Mut, Amun's consort and the patron goddess of Thebes. Behind Mut's temple a lake was excavated. The pharaoh then laid out a pathway from the Precinct of Mut to Luxor, and lined it with gardens.

Amenhotep's Queen, Tiye

About 1,000 yards (915m) south of the giant statue of Amenhotep lie two depressions that once constituted an artificial lake excavated by Amenhotep III for his queen and favorite wife, Tiye. According to tradition, this great lake, on which the royal couple would sail in a royal barge, was one mile (1.6km) long and a thousand feet (305m) wide. The two depressions are the only remnant of the palace that the pharaoh built for his wife. Unfortunately, the palaces of the New Kingdom pharaohs, unlike their stone temples and tombs, did not last the ages because they were made of mud brick. As a result, the evidence of their everyday life has, in most instances, eroded away.

The relationship between Amenhotep III and Tiye has all the signs of a compatible match, a relationship between equals, which is surprising because Tiye seems to have been a commoner, not related to the king at all. This intriguing departure from custom was perhaps due to Amenhotep's desire to escape from the control of the priests of Amun, who had traditionally had a hand in determining the brides of the pharaoh. Since the reign of Tuthmosis I, the power of these priests had been growing, and by the time of Amenhotep it might have become so great that the pharaoh felt the priests needed to be thwarted somehow. What better way to demonstrate his independence than to reject their choice of a bride by seeking out a woman of nonroyal background?

If such a rift did exist between this pharaoh and the priests of Amun, it would go a long way toward explaining Amenhotep IV's (1353–1335) utter rejection and subjugation of them. Whatever the politi-

cal or religious motivations of Amenhotep III's marriage, Tiye seems to have been a true partner to her husband. Her name or image almost always appears with his on reliefs and sculptures. She also appears on Amenhotep's commemorative scarabs, pieces of jewelry bearing a synopsis of an important event on their underside that were apparently distributed throughout the empire to "advertise" the event. She was even present at diplomatic functions such as the one where Amenhotep greeted his latest wife, Ghilukhepa, daughter of King Shuttarna of Mitanni, when she arrived with an impressive entourage in Egypt. Most important, Tiye received letters from foreign rulers that seem to indicate that they considered her to be an influential advisor to her husband. Whatever the case, Amenhotep paid her the ultimate compliment by building a temple to her at Sedeinga, below the Third Cataract in Nubia, where she was worshiped as a local manifestation of the goddess Hathor. She survived the king and served as an advisor to her son, Akhenaten, whose radical religious reforms would shake the country and make him an incredibly powerful ruler, though not always a popular one.

Left: Dated to about 1300 B.C., this bronze mirror features a handle consisting of the head of Hathor and a stylized lotus flower.
Below: Originally meant to portray Amenhotep III, this seated statue was altered by Rameses II, who had Amenhotep's signature removed and his own substituted. The statue, made from granodiorite, is in the Louvre.

Akhenaten

Amenhotep III and Tiye's son, Amenhotep IV, or Akhenaten, would become the most famous Egyptian ruler after Cleopatra VII. The reason for this is probably that he seems, at least in the popular mind today, to have rebelled against the polytheistic religion of the Egyptians and adopted instead a monotheistic religion, which holds greater appeal for most people today.

His goal seemed to be to elevate his new conception of god high above that of the traditional worship of Amun. He worshipped Aten, a manifestation of Amun that represented the sun at its apex. Aten was the orb of the sun, the simplest and purest manifestation of this great source of life, uncluttered by the manipulations and theology of Amun. Emanating from this orb were several rays, each ending in an *ankh*, the Egyptian symbol of life.

To a large degree, these theological revisions may have been sparked by Amenhotep IV's desire to destroy the power of the priests of Amun, against whom his father may also have conspired. In the fifth year of his reign he suddenly closed the temples to Amun and Amun-Re, took away the income of their priests, and erased Amun's name and that of other gods from royal monuments, even when that meant ordering the destruction of his father's cartouche when it occurred in conjunction with the name of Amun.

Akhetaten, the New Capital

But it did not end there. Amenhotep IV decided that he and his court could no longer be contaminated by the religious impurity of Thebes, and he moved the capital of Egypt 300 miles (480km) north to Akhetaten, or Horizon of Aten. This site, now called Tell el Amarna, lies in a huge bay on the eastern side of the Nile. There had been no previous building on this site, so Amenhotep—or Akhenaten, Beloved of Aten, as he now styled himself—felt completely free of any contaminating influences. The city he built there did not survive his death, however, and the site quickly became deserted and was never built on again. This is fortunate for Egyptologists, who have here a time capsule of New Kingdom urban life uncluttered by later building.

The center of the town was based around two great buildings: the Temple of Aten and, slightly to the south, the Great Palace. The Great Temple was unique among Egyptian houses of worship because instead of a closed sanctuary it featured a huge court open to the sky. After entering through a double wall, the visitor passed four giant statues of Akhenaten and

came into an open area filled with several hundred raised platforms of stone or mud brick. Their purpose is not clear to us today, but they may have been offering sites for people considered too impure to enter the main sanctuary. A relief found at Amarna pictures these low tables piled high with fruits and flowers.

Some evidence suggests that Akhenaten believed that only he and his beautiful wife, Nefertiti, were sufficiently holy to sacrifice to Aten in this open sanctuary—several reliefs depict the pharaoh and his queen sacrificing directly to Aten using no tables or paraphernalia at all.

Left: Akhenaten and Nefertiti play with three of their children under the rays of the Sun Disk, or Aten. The picture is unique for the informality in the portrayal of the royal family.

The Great Palace consisted of four open courts, one in each corner, with hypostyle halls between them. The palace sat on a low hill overlooking the Nile and had a number of descending terraces filled with trees and gardens that extended down to a royal wharf. The private house of the king was directly across the thoroughfare from the palace, and the pharaoh could come and go across a convenient bridge.

Directly east of the Great Palace is the "Record Office," so called because excavators in A.D. 1887 discovered there a large cache of cuneiform documents from the various royal courts of Mesopotamia. This collection of letters outlines some disturbing aspects of Egyptian foreign policy during the reign of Akhenaten. The traditional allies of Egypt, the Mitanni princes, were facing attack from the Hittites under an especially active ruler named Shuppilumash, who was gradually pushing the borders of his kingdom

southward. The Mitanni princes wrote letters to Akhenaten begging for troops and support, but Akhenaten apparently was too involved in his social reform to respond. By the end of Akhenaten's reign, northern Syria was in Hittite hands and the coastal cities of Sidon, Tyre, and Byblos were under Hittite domination.

Meanwhile, in the beautiful new city of Akhetaten, other changes were afoot. Artistically, the pharaoh was fostering a radical change. There seems to have been a deliberate switch from the stiff formalism of earlier Egyptian art to a completely naturalistic representation of the world and the people in it. No longer, for instance, was the pharaoh depicted as a strong, virile, young man with a youthful face and a bodybuilder's physique—Akhenaten's artists portrayed him as a potbellied, stoop-shouldered weakling. Instead of stiff formal poses of the pharaoh and the queen, as had been the rule in Egyptian art since the Old Kingdom, Akhenaten and Nefertiti are shown in intimate poses as a loving family surrounded by their six daughters. In a portrait dating from shortly after the death of their daughter Meketaten, the whole royal family is shown gathered around the young girl's body, heads sadly bowed in grief, in a very human display of emotion.

Nefertiti

It is this extreme naturalism that has been responsible for the fame of Akhenaten's wife. Normally, in Egyptian art, all wives of pharaohs appeared beautiful, whether they really were or not. But since the famous portrait busts of Nefertiti were most likely created with accuracy in mind, we can assume that she was indeed a breathtakingly beautiful woman. One portrait bust of her, found in the workshop of a sculptor named Tuthmosis in the

southern part of Akhetaten, is perhaps the best known representation of an ancient Egyptian, and probably one of the most reproduced statues in the world. This departure from standard artistic style was one of the few lasting legacies of Akhenaten's rule, for it is still evident, in a slightly modified form, in the artwork of one of Akhenaten's successors, the famous Tutankhamun.

Akhenaten has been portrayed by various writers in a number of different and contradictory ways: to some he was a heroic religious revolutionary, the inspirer of the monotheism of the ancient Hebrews; to others he was a weak ineffective homosexual or perhaps a woman disguised as a male. There are statues of him that seem feminine, and some observers have assumed that this was a slam. Others say he was just effeminate. Most historians agree that his uncle Horemheb murdered him, although they differ on why.

One theory is that he acted as an agent of jealous Amun priests, while another is that he lusted for Nefertiti. The legends and suppositions are endless, and probably all untrue—and they don't end with the pharaoh. His queen, Nefertiti, has suffered in much the same way.

She has been portrayed as the instigator of Akhenaten's monotheistic heresy and, alternately, as a victim of it. She is sometimes depicted as the murderess of her husband, or as a murdered victim herself. It has been supposed that she was secretly the lover of the sculptor Tuthmosis, caught in an act of infidelity and murdered as a result. Or perhaps she was simply a pretty face around whom swirled the plots and counterplots of a wickedly decadent court. The best guess is that Nefertiti, who was always an ardent supporter of her husband, died before he did. Desperate for an heir who was male, the pharaoh then married his daughter Ankhesenpaaten, who bore him another daughter, who was given the tongue-twisting name Ankhhesenpattentasherit, or Ankhesenpaaten "Junior." When Akhenaten died in 1335—we do not know how—he was succeeded by his half-brother Semenkhare, who reigned for only two years before he died and was succeeded by his brother, the famous Tutankhamun.

Left: Probably the most famous portrait bust in the world, this head of Nefertiti was found in the workshop of a sculptor named Tuthmosis at Tell el-Amarna. **Below:** A small limestone statue depicts Pharaoh Akhenaten with one of his daughters seated on his lap.

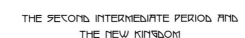

TUTANKHAMUN

Tutankhamun (1330–1320) took steps to return Egypt to the old ways and was rewarded for it. He reopened all the temples of Amun and the other gods. He appointed new priests of Amun because a shortage apparently existed at this time. He did not, however, eliminate references to Aten; he merely returned the god to his status as one of the many manifestations of the sun.

Though the priests of Amun hated Akhenaten, they did not get their chance for revenge during the reign of Tutankhamun. The young king continued for a time to live in Akhetaten, and apparently took no action against the tomb or funerary temple of Akhenaten. Nor does there seem to have been any act of disrespect toward the innovative pharaoh under Aya, Tutankhamun's successor (1323–1319). This did not occur until the reign of Horemheb (1319–1307), when Akhenaten's beautiful city was destroyed, his nearby tomb desecrated, and his name ripped off numerous monuments.

Why the sixteen-year span between the death of Akhenaten and the sudden, furious destruction of his monuments and name? It seems out of character for Horemheb, formerly a trusted advisor and general for Akhenaten, to have encouraged or allowed such behavior. Perhaps through some unchronicled political maneuverings within the court, the priests of Amun finally were able to regain enough leverage to get the new pharaoh to go along with this wholesale destruction. Whoever was responsible certainly made a complete job of it, even instituting the custom of dating events from the reign of Akhenaten using the phrase "in the year of the Criminal of Akhetaten."

KING TUT'S TOMB

In any event, the young king Tutankhamun seems to have pulled the country back together again politically and to have begun to reassert the prestige of the Egyptian empire in Syria and Palestine. Perhaps the nation was grateful, and that is why his burial was especially rich. Historians used to assume that Tutankhamun, being a comparatively minor king, had been buried with only a small amount of the wealth that would normally have graced the tomb of a truly successful, long-ruling monarch, but a reexamination of the tombs of Egypt seems to reveal that King Tut's was the exception, and that most other burials held much less treasure.

Regardless, when archaeologist Howard Carter opened the tomb in A.D. 1922, he found that, although tomb robbers had discovered the tomb in antiquity, they had mys-

teriously left most of its furnishings. The world was awestruck by the richness of the tomb. Especially impressive was the goldwork, which included solid gold fly whisks, a dagger hilt, small gold-plated shrines, a tiny gold statue of the scorpion goddess Serket (to guard the king's canopic jar, which held his viscera), and the solid gold mummy case, which weighs nearly a ton. This magnificent object, which bears a realistic image of the king's face, is decorated with lapis lazuli, carnelian, and turquoise.

Besides gold, there is stunning stonework, especially in alabaster. There is, for instance, a charming alabaster boat with an ibex head on the prow. Kneeling in the prow is a lovely girl holding a lotus flower to her chest, while in the back is a tiny figure of a dwarf who is poling the boat along. Numerous examples of Egyptian furniture were also present, including cabinets made of red cedar wood and ebony, four beds, and two thrones decorated with gold and paste simulations of

Above: On a piece of pectoral jewelry made from gold and lapis lazuli, a figure of the king stands between a vulture and a cobra, signs of royalty. The item is designed to be worn suspended from the neck, resting on the upper chest. **Left:** Four small sarcophagi, miniature replicas of the larger mummy case in the burial chamber, each about 15⅜ inches (39cm) high and made of gold, carnelian, and glass paste, held the king's viscera—the liver, lungs, stomach, and intestines.

lapis lazuli and turquoise. Finally, there was the young pharaoh's war chariot, probably never used in actual battle—decorated with panels of wood bearing figures of defeated Nubian and Syrian foes made of stucco covered with beaten gold. Besides the wealth of gold and beautiful minor objects, the tomb featured a number of wall paintings portraying the departed ruler being greeted by Anubis and Isis, in the presence of Osiris, the lord of the dead, and pictures of funerary boats. These paintings are in the Amarna style, showing the king and his associates (but not the gods) with pot bellies and generally flabby bodies.

One of the most endearing objects found in the tomb was a small gold-plated shrine, whose sides

Above: In the center of this earring a figure of the king is flanked by two cobras, with a hawk above his head. Measuring about 2 inches by 4 inches (5 by 10cm), the earrings were suspended by a thick string that would have required an exceptionally large hole in the ear lobe.
Right: The famous gold funerary mask of Tutankhamun was an exact image of the young king. The blue details on the headdress, or *nemset*, are made from glass paste, but the blue of the eyebrows and eyes is lapis lazuli. The *nemset* is decorated with the cobra and vulture, two animals that represent the king's power and were always associated with the pharaoh.

giant doorway on the east side of Karnak and placed on either side two colossal statues of himself as Osiris.

Across the Nile from the great Karnak complex, Rameses II built his mortuary temple, the Ramesseum. This huge complex included not only his funerary temple but also an array of storehouses, dwellings, and shops for artisans. There were also more than twenty large, vaulted granaries designed to hold enough wheat and barley to maintain a temple staff of about 240 for two years. Finally, there were smaller, more specialized storehouses for wine, honey, and oil. Money was still not being used in Egypt at this time, and payment for services was usually in commodities that could be eaten.

The funerary temple itself had a large pylon at its front that gave way on to a large, open-air court surrounded by columns. In the center of this court stood a massive 66-foot (20m) statue of Rameses II that weighed 1,000 tons. Another open court nearby had its own statue of the pharaoh, again depicted as Osiris. Behind this open court a hypostyle hall led through three small colonnaded halls to a sanctuary.

Behind the Ramesseum, a tall cliff runs north and south. On the other side of this natural barrier is the famous Valley of the Kings, where, at the same time the Ramesseum was being built, the pharaoh oversaw the construction of his tomb. This tomb, dug straight into solid rock, was 324 feet (99m) long, and the reliefs lining its walls are some of the finest in

Egypt. There was, however, at least one screwup in the creation of the tomb—at one point, one of the workmen misspelled Rameses II's name, and the error was hastily covered over with plaster.

The workmen who built the Ramesseum and the pharaoh's tomb lived in Deir el Medina, a worker's village founded by Tuthmosis I to house the special artisans and workers that built the tombs and memorials around Thebes. This town was similar in design to Kahun, where the workers who built the

eight of his children (who must have been fortunate indeed to attract the attention of their father, for Rameses supposedly sired 140 children). And if all this wasn't enough, another sign of Rameses' colossal egotism can be viewed on the outside of this temple: the statue of the sun god Re Herakhty cut into the rock above the door is only about half the size of the statues of the pharaoh.

For once, however, Rameses outreached himself. Three of the figures cut into the outside of the great temple were sculpted out of rock that had a fault. Soon after the statues were completed, pieces of them began to break away. Still, the temple is most impressive. It is cut into a red sandstone cliff face and goes back 200 feet (61m) to the sanctuary. Inside are stat-

ues, a great hall, an anteroom, and several side chapels. The temple is oriented toward the rising sun, so that twice a year the sun's rays shine all the way along the 200-foot corridor to illuminate the statues of Rameses and of the god Atum sitting in the sanctuary.

The walls of this great temple are covered with hieroglyphic inscriptions and reliefs that glorify Rameses and his many victories over the enemies of Egypt. Chief among those is his defeat of the Hittites at Kadesh in 1286. The irony is that although Rameses' relief at Abu Simbel presents Kadesh as an overwhelming victory, the discovery of a Hittite description of the battle makes it clear that it was in fact a strategic defeat, and the pharaoh was fortunate to escape with the remnant of his army.

A Dangerous Time

Rameses lived a long and happy life. In his later years, he grew extremely obese because of his unrestrained eating and drinking, and in his final years he was too senile to rule. He turned control of his government over to his son Merneptah (1224–1214), who proved to be an able ruler in a dangerous time.

By the end of the thirteenth millennium, on the frontiers especially, the enemies of Egypt had grown strong and were attracted to the country by the wealth it had stolen from others. To the west, the Libyans had formed an alliance of sorts with a group called the Sea Peoples—a collection of people from all over the Mediterranean—and were once more attacking the oases. And although Merneptah defeated this alliance in several great battles, there were other enemies. The Nubians began fresh attacks on the Egyptian frontiers to the south, and the Hittites and Assyrians began to chip away at the frontiers of the empire in Syria.

As if these attacks from outside weren't damaging enough, within Egypt itself there was civil war. The death of Merneptah brought forth a succession of weak rulers, and the Nineteenth Dynasty ended with the death of Twosre (1198–1196), a female pharaoh. The succeeding Twentieth Dynasty (1196–1070) was filled with men who were not of the caliber of earlier pharaohs, and they faced times that would have taxed a Tuthmosis III, as wave after wave of invaders tried their luck against the Egyptian frontiers.

The decline in the military fortunes of Egypt was reflected in the architecture of the era, most of which is a mere shadow of the earlier buildings and monuments. Only Rameses III (1194–1163) built anything to match the work of earlier pharaohs, and his mortuary temple at Medinet Habu was just a smaller copy of Rameses II's efforts. In short, the dynamism that had made the New Kingdom so remarkably great was gone.

Left: The end of the rose granite sarcophagus of Rameses III. The beautiful female winged figure is the goddess Isis, a special protector of the deceased. Rameses III's mummy was unfortunately plundered from this sarcophagus, but it survived and was reburied by mortuary priests of the Twenty-first Dynasty (1070–945 B.C.). It remained hidden for nearly three thousand years until Charles Edwin Wilbour, an avid collector of Egyptian antiquities, discovered it in A.D. 1881. **Pages 156–157:** The tomb of Nefretari, the favorite wife of Rameses II, lies in the Valley of the Queens, which is about a mile south of the more famous Valley of the Kings and contains the tombs of seventy wives and children of the pharaohs of the Nineteenth and Twentieth Dynasties.

Below: The golden seal of Pharaoh Horemheb shows his cartouche. He was commander-in-chief of the army under Akhenaten, and his wife Mudnodjme may have been a sister of Nefertiti, Akhenaten's beautiful wife.

THE MILITARY BASIS FOR THE NEW KINGDOM

The great wealth and success of Egypt under the New Kingdom would not have been possible without its firm military base—of all the empires of the sixteenth century B.C. only Egypt had a full-time army. For many young men, the New Kingdom army became the career of preference because it promised advancement. Horemheb, for instance, started life as a common soldier and ended as pharaoh.

The need for a professional army had become apparent during the long war to dislodge the Hyksos from the Delta, which lasted from about 1570 to about 1550, and the subsequent expansion of Egypt into modern-day Israel, Lebanon, and southwestern Syria. By this time, both the Hittites and the peoples of southwest Asia had adopted the chariot as the backbone of their armies, and the Egyptians were forced to follow suit. They also modified chariot warfare to include specially trained and specially armed infantry forces.

Chariot tactics of the sixteenth through the eleventh centuries were built around the idea that well-trained archers armed with composite bows made of laminated wood and bone could deliver a deadly barrage of missile fire

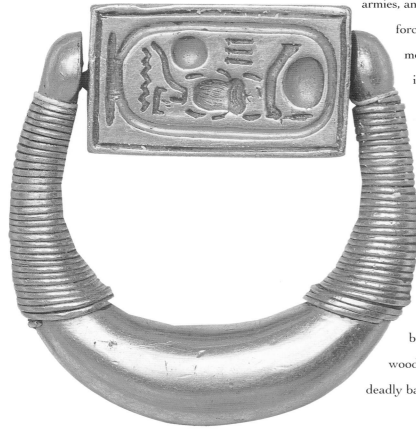

against infantry forces armed mainly with clubs, axes, and spears. The training, of course, was paramount, for it is extremely difficult to accurately fire a bow from a bouncing platform traveling at high speed. Performance was further hindered by the heavy armor of the individual firing the composite bow—a jacket made of hundreds of pieces of bronze sewn on a fitted piece of leather, a conical metal cap, and a high metal collar—which was necessary to protect the chariot archer from the missile weapons of the enemy's infantry line. The archer took no hand in guiding the chariot; that task was entrusted to a driver whose only protection was a thick wooden shield held on his left arm and the armored body of the archer standing to his right. Contrary to popular conception, the chariot did not crash into the infantry line—such a tactic would have been suicidal for the horses—but instead approached the line with the archer firing continuously, then suddenly wheeled to the right (so the driver's shield would offer maximum protection) and beat a hasty retreat in order to gain enough distance to make another charge.

However, Egyptian charioteers seldom attacked a line of infantry, for they had a well-trained and rigidly disciplined infantry for that. The Egyptians also had a much larger pool of manpower than any of their potential enemies, so their armies preferred infantry battles. The main goal of the Egyptians was to protect their own infantry from enemy chariot attacks. The usual foes for Egyptian chariots, therefore, were other chariots. When charioteers went up against other lines of charioteers, the tactics were radically different from those used in fighting infantry. Since relatively wide intervals had to be maintained between chariots, it was entirely possible for a charioteer to drive right through an opposing line. As the two lines approached

wooden shield carried on the left arm.

By the time of Tuthmosis IV (1400–1392), however, there had been some changes in both arms and protection for the body. Now, in addition to the battle ax, soldiers were armed with the *khopesh*, an oddly shaped bronze sword with a pronounced right angle in the middle of the blade. This strange right angle gave the weapon slightly more weight in a downward swing, and made the *khopesh* an effective slashing weapon. As for body armor, the Egyptian infantry not only wore the stiffened linen crotch protector they had always worn, but also carried a larger wooden shield and wore thick, stiffened linen padding around their middles and over both shoulders. Lightly armed as these soldiers were, they were consistently better armed than the men they fought. The key to Egyptian success was not only that they were trained to fight in disciplined units that responded to commands as a group, but that all were uniformly armed at the expense of the state, making resupply and repair of weapons and implementation of battle tactics easier. Most of the other infantry they fought against were nothing more than hastily organized militia which brought to the battlefield a variety of weapons and armor and little organization.

Egyptian archers, whose bodies were also protected by nothing more than the stiffened linen, were effective for much the same reasons. Although the Egyptians began their conquests using archers armed with only a stave bow made of a single piece of wood,

Left: In a relief from the walls of Sethos I's temple at Abydos, the young Rameses II hunts lions with a bow and arrows. The motif of pharaohs hunting lions was common throughout the New Kingdom. **Below:** Recovered from his tomb, the base of Tutankhamun's fly whisk is made of wood covered with gold, and the top curved edge has thirty tiny holes that once held ostrich feathers. The scene on the front depicts the king hunting ostriches from a racing chariot. The other side shows the king returning in triumph with two servants carrying slain ostriches in front of the chariot.

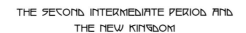

each other, archers on both sides would shoot as many arrows as possible. When the two lines met, they would pass through each other, then wheel around to repeat the same tactic until one side or the other had lost too many vehicles to continue.

Soldiers and Archers

New Kingdom infantry was divided into two entirely different groups: assault troops and archers. In the early New Kingdom, each soldier was armed mainly with a bronze ax and a dagger. These soldiers wore no armor or padding of any kind, except for a long piece of stiffened linen that covered the groin area and a

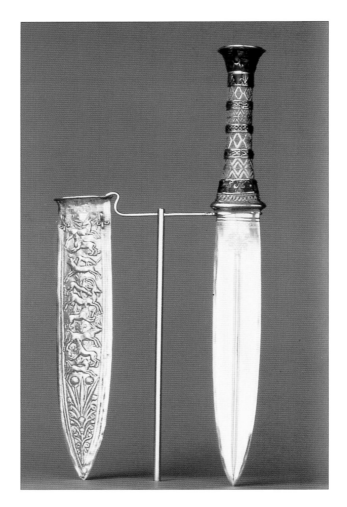

chariots and keep them away from the infantry, although the composite bows of the Egyptian infantry could usually deal with a line of attacking chariots if the archers had time to deploy in a battle line. Also, most chariots of the Hittites and Mitanni were much heavier than Egyptian chariots. This made it more sensible to fight them from a distance, first rushing in to discharge arrows, then falling back out of range before swooping in close again. The heavy enemy chariots often could not catch the lighter Egyptian ones.

In short, Egypt had a winning combination of superior weaponry and professional troops who spent their lives training for battle. Add to this the fact that the Egyptians spent a great deal of time on logistics — supplying a field army — and the result was an almost unbeatable military machine.

The Battle of Megiddo

the bows were produced to a common standard, and their uniformity made them effective. Later in the New Kingdom period, the state armed its archers with the expensive composite bow; none of Egypt's enemies were wealthy enough to supply all of their archers with this weapon. The range of the composite bow was over 200 yards (183m), three times that of arrows fired from the simple stave bows of Egypt's enemies.

The preferred tactic of the Egyptian army was to advance the infantry toward the enemy under an arching overhead fire from the Egyptian bowmen. Usually this rain of arrows would disrupt an enemy line enough so that when the infantry reached the line, it was a relatively easy matter to break through. The Egyptian chariots normally remained on the flanks of the infantry or ranged ahead of the ground troops to act as scouts. Their main function was to attack enemy

Though we know that the Egyptians won many battles, we do not have many details. Apparently, victories were so frequent that there was no interest in recounting how they were won. Successful commanders instead concentrated on the booty they brought back, and the walls of their tombs are covered not with battle accounts but with lists of loot, an easily understandable measure of success.

In all of Egyptian history, we have detailed accounts of only two battles, and in each, historians have to make assumptions because the reason for victory is so often stated as nothing more than the personal bravery of the pharaoh.

In about 1452, Tuthmosis III's army advanced along the Sinai coast road to Gaza, then moved north along the coast to Yehem, near modern Haifa, Israel, where it paused. About 10 miles (16km) to the east lay

Megiddo, a strong fortress occupied by a confederation of Asians. Between the two armies lay the Carmel Ridge, a spur of Mount Carmel. There were three passes through this barrier, one that came out slightly to the north of Meggido at Zefti, another that left the ridge to the south of Taanach, and a middle route that came out directly in front of Megiddo. The northern and southern routes were more open and flat, and so were more accessible to the movement of an army. But the Asians, unbeknownst to the Egyptians, had massed their army at Taanach, perhaps because they expected the pharaoh's forces there. The middle route lay open, because it was so steep and narrow that the Asians probably did not think it possible for an army to pass through.

The Egyptian army advanced from Yehem to a small village named Aruna and stopped while Tuthmosis consulted his officers, who argued for either the northern or the southern route. They feared the middle route, because the Asians could discover them, block the pass and annihilate the Egyptians in the narrow defile. After listening to his commanders, the pharaoh decided to take the dangerous middle route. There is no explanation for this risky decision. Perhaps Tuthmosis had some military intelligence that told him the enemy was massed at Taanach. Or he could have assumed they would ignore the middle route since it seemed unnavigable.

The Egyptians' clever move caught the Asians completely by surprise, and as the pharaoh's army emerged from the mountain defile, apparently having stopped just out of sight to reassemble their chariots, the enemy fell back to try to form a line between the attackers and the city. It was too late in the day to fight, however, and both armies waited for the morning. This seems rather anticlimactic, but nighttime

assaults on chariots over rough ground did not occur in ancient warfare.

The next morning, Tuthmosis ordered the attack and led it from the center of the line against a formation of Asian chariots. Perhaps still unnerved, the enemy broke and fled back to the city before the pharaoh and his troops even reached their line. The people in the city were too afraid to open the gates, so instead they tied together pieces of clothing and used these "ropes" to draw the soldiers up to safety. The Asians had abandoned their chariots and camp on the plain and, to the immense displeasure of Tuthmosis, his troops stopped to plunder the Asian camp instead of pursuing the enemy to the walls. To capture the town, Tuthmosis had to lay siege. The Egyptians dug a moat around Megiddo and cut down trees to build a stockade behind it so that the city's people were completely cut off from escape.

Above: A relief on Hatshepsut's Temple at Deir el Bahri shows a group of Egyptian soldiers armed with spears and shields. Egyptian soldiers traditionally fought with very little armor. Their shields were made of wooden slats covered with either painted linen or a distinctive color of animal hide to designate the soldiers' regiments.

Eventually, the city surrendered, and Tuthmosis practiced remarkable clemency toward the prisoners given the period of history. He allowed the soldiers to return to their homes unmolested, on foot or on donkeys. He did, however, take their horses and weapons as booty. On the reliefs at Karnak it is proudly stated that Tuthmosis brought home 2,041 horses from Megiddo.

The battle at Megiddo marked the beginning of a long period of Egyptian expansion in the Middle East under the Eighteenth-Dynasty pharaohs Tuthmosis III, his son Amenhotep II, and his grandson Amenhotep III.

Battling the Hittites

Sethos I, the first important pharaoh of the Nineteenth Dynasty, continued this tradition of conquest. In 1302 he sought out the Hittite king Muwatallis north of the city of Kadesh, on the Orontes River in present-day Syria. Frustratingly, we know only that Sethos won, not how he effected this victory. We have a complete list of tribute, but not a single detail of the battle itself. Following the battle, Sethos concluded a treaty with Muwatallis, and it appears that this sector of the Egyptian frontier was quiet for another sixteen years.

However, in 1286, Sethos' son Rameses II again led an army north toward Kadesh. Apparently, despite Sethos' earlier victory, Muwatallis and his Hittites had returned in force to make another attempt to extend their border south into territory the Egyptians had claimed as part of their empire. Rameses advanced out of Egypt and up the eastern coast of the Mediterranean to approximately the modern border between Syria and Israel, where he conquered the Amurruians, an ally of the Hittites.

Rameses was not all that interested in battling these people, but he knew such an attack would force Muwatallis to attack him. Since the campaigning season was over, however, both sides had to wait until the next year. The modern world often forgets how dependent the ancient world was on seasonal crops that produced a much lower yield than today's varieties; after six months in the field, an ancient army would have used up its supplies and thus needed to return home to restock.

The next year, Rameses II led an army directly for Kadesh, now called Tall An-Nabi Mind. This city in southwestern Syria controlled access to the Syrian Plain, the great open area that commanded the route into northern Syria and the heart of the Hittite Empire. Rameses apparently aimed at nothing less than the complete subjugation of the Hittites. Defeating the Hittite army on its own ground, however, would not be easy. Here the Hittites would be close to their own supply bases, while the Egyptians had to depend on a supply trail extending back to Egypt, which meant that they had to transport supplies across the eastern Mediterranean.

Another year later, both armies gathered around Kadesh for a battle. The Battle of Kadesh, one of the most famous in all history, clearly demonstrated the power and ability of the Egyptian military machine, even when commanded by a general who was, to put it bluntly, incredibly slow-witted. Rameses entered the campaign with an unrealistic faith in himself and a contemptuous attitude toward the Hittite army. His pride and arrogance exposed the Egyptians to a tactical situation that very nearly resulted in their destruction. Only the technical superiority of the Egyptian chariots, matched with the skill of their crews, turned near disaster into a slim tactical victory for the Egyptian army.

As the battle began, the Egyptian army approached Kadesh from two directions. The main force left Egypt at the end of April and reached the approximate position of modern Haifa one month later, then turned inland toward the Orontes River. At the same time, a second force made up of elite chariot troops and infantry proceeded along the coast and secured the allegiance of the coastal cities. These troops were supposed to join with the principal army for the final attack against Kadesh. The rest of the pharaoh's army moved east until they struck the Orontes and then turned north along the banks of that river and headed toward Kadesh, the last reported position of Muwatallis and his Hittites. Just as the Egyptians began to cross the Orontes, however, Egyptian scouts brought in two Bedouins, who claimed to be deserters from the Hittite army. Brought before Rameses, they eagerly volunteered the information that Muwatallis and his army were nowhere near Kadesh. In fact, they said, he was nearly 100 miles (160km) north at Aleppo, deep in Hittite territory. This suited Rameses' preconceptions exactly. The gods seemed to be favoring him.

Without confirming the information of the two men through reconnaissance of his own, the pharaoh violated the most basic principle of war and divided his

Below: The north wall of the hypostyle hall of Sethos I at Karnak portrays the pharaoh in his chariot pursuing defeated Hittites and Libyans. While the chariot driver might be unarmored, the fighter in the chariot would have armor made of bronze scales stitched to a leather jacket as well as a high conical helmet made of bronze.

Above: A relief from the Second Pylon of the Ramesseum depicts an Egyptian chariot crew engaged in battle. Both crewmen are looking back over their shoulders as if they are being pursued. The man with the shield has raised it as if to repel arrows.

probably never know which scenario was true. In any event, modern students of tactics still study this campaign to draw valuable lessons about how a commander needs to be cautious in the gathering of military intelligence.

Rameses and his small detachment swept forward and halted just north of Kadesh. The Amun Division came up behind him and began to establish a camp several hundred yards to the south of the pharaoh's position. Muwatallis, as it turned out, was not at Aleppo but was waiting with a group of his chariots behind Kadesh and out of sight of the Egyptian army. As the Re Division moved north, the Hittite

army. With a small contingent of household troops, he sprinted north toward Kadesh, ordering one quarter of the army, the Division of Amun, to catch up as quickly as possible with him. The other divisions, named after the gods Re, Ptah, and Seth, were far in the rear of the line of march; they were ordered to catch up when they could. No explanation exists about why Rameses felt the need to dash forward with only a portion of his army, but as he did so, a gap of about four miles (6½km) opened between the Amun Division and the other three divisions. Rameses had placed his army in a tactically dangerous position.

Although many historians suspect that the two Bedouins were actually spies for Muwatallis, it is equally possible that they were just overawed by the presence of Rameses and told the king what they thought he wanted to hear. Unfortunately, we will

king launched his chariots across the shallow Orontes River directly into the flank of the Egyptians. The Hittites were on them before they had time to form a defensive line, and the soldiers of the Re Division broke formation and ran for the Amun Division. Muwatallis drove through the remnants of the Re Division, swung northwest, and hit the Amun Division in its right flank. The surprise attack shattered the Amun Division as well, and in less than thirty minutes the Hittites had destroyed the cohesion of one half of the Egyptian army.

Meanwhile, Rameses, still in his camp, did the only thing possible. He sent messengers to tell the Ptah and Seth Divisions to come up as quickly as possible, and with his small group of personal guards he launched a chariot attack on the Hittites. This was an incredibly courageous maneuver, and in view of the situation it was the only thing he could do. Outnumbered by about twenty to one, Rameses led his chariots into the thickest part of the Hittite battle line. At least six times, the Egyptian chariots crashed through the Hittites' chariots, circled around, and attacked again. It seems impossible, but they slowly began to inflict substantial casualties on the enemy. The key to their success probably lay in the utter disorganization of the Hittite army by this time and in the superiority of the Egyptian chariots over the Hittites'.

When the pharaoh and his small group of chariots attacked, the Hittites were divided into three disjointed groups. One group was busy finishing off the remnants of the Re Division, another was slashing its way through the Amun Division's camp, and a third had ceased fighting altogether and was plundering the Amun camp. The fact that the Hittites were scattered resulted in the Egyptians' not having to fight the enemy at full strength; they were able to concentrate on the group near the Amun camp.

Muwatallis, however, was no fool; he saw how the situation was going and ordered more chariots from behind Kadesh to cross the Orontes and engage the Egyptians. As this second Hittite horde bore down on Ramesses' men, a small group of chariots that the pharaoh had dispatched days before to overawe the cities farther west suddenly appeared on the battlefield. To the Hittites, this must have seemed a miracle; their second wave of chariots was driven back across the Orontes. The Hittites retreated.

Rameses had won, but it had been a Pyrrhic victory. The Egyptian army, unable to maintain its offensive posture, retreated back into Egypt. Still, the defeat of the Hittites was enough to secure a treaty that established a border and brought about a cessation of hostilities. Except for sporadic raids back and forth, the Egyptians and the Hittites maintained peaceful relations from then on. A Hittite bride even came to Egypt and became one of the dozens of wives of Rameses. It was good luck for the Egyptians that, soon after this battle of Kadesh, the Assyrians became a major power in Mesopotamia and threatened the Hittites on their home ground. The Battle of Kadesh had saved the Egyptian empire—at least for the time being—until the next, newer, stronger enemy was ready to fight.

Below: Among the reliefs carved on the Second Pylon of the Ramesseum were these representations of chariots rolling over the dead bodies of the slain enemy, a favorite subject of such carvings throughout Egypt.

LITERATURE AND MEDICINE IN THE NEW KINGDOM

In addition to its astounding monuments and great armies, the New Kingdom also created impressive monuments of another kind. Ancient Egypt's New Kingdom witnessed the production not only of impressive theological works but a popular literature that people read for pleasure. These advances were matched by accomplishments in the field of medicine, for dozens of medical texts were written during this period. While some of them were merely new editions of medical works from the Old and Middle Kingdoms, the majority seem to be specific to the new era.

The largest Egyptian medical papyrus, the Ebers Papyrus, is a product of the New Kingdom.

Although archaeologists are not certain of its exact origins, it appears to have come from the tomb of a New Kingdom doctor and to have been written during the reign of Amenhotep I (1525–1505). Its 110 pages are filled with an almost haphazard collection of medical problems. Stomach ailments, intestinal worms, diseases of the anus and urinary tract, eye ailments, burns, and diseases of the tongue, eye, ear, nose, and throat are just some of the subjects considered in this document. There is also a section dealing with basic anatomy that describes the heart, liver, testicles, bladder, and major blood vessels.

The author of the Ebers Papyrus seems to have been especially interested in diseases of the eye. This is not surprising, since ancient Egyptians were invariably susceptible to eye diseases because of the intense sunlight and blowing sand of their desert environment. According to the papyrus, swelling and red-

ness of the eyes can be treated with black or green eye paint made from powdered galena and malachite. The treatment for blindness includes washing the eye with the "water of a pig's eye," which may be the author's words for the aqueous humor of the pig's eye. An eye that is swollen shut and from which pus is oozing should be treated with applications of pig bile. To combat night blindness, the Ebers author recommends covering the eye with liver; the fact that liver, a rich source of vitamin A and a recognized modern treatment for night blindness, was chosen is purely coincidental. Eyes that are excessively watery, a problem that would no doubt be aggravated by blowing sand, should be treated with an application of ground lapis lazuli and crocodile dung. For trachoma, an especially prevalent eye disease in Egypt, the recommended treatment involved the application of the bile of a turtle's liver, ground acacia leaves, or even ground granite.

Interestingly enough, bad teeth or gums are not discussed in any Egyptian medical papyrus, although mummies show evidence of ground-down teeth, and gum disease is also prevalent. Most of this periodontal disease was so advanced that excavators could have removed the teeth simply by yanking them out with the fingers. Again, the desert environment was certainly a factor, as well as the fact that barley and emmer wheat were ground in flat stone dishes with a stone grinder so there was always stone grit in the bread the Egyptians ate.

In addition to its many medical writings, the New Kingdom produced a vast number of copies of *The Book of the Dead.* This was apparently a major industry, for the books were produced on long papyrus rolls with blank spaces left for decedents' names. Most of these scrolls were placed in the coffins with the mummies. Almost all of the pictures that show the dead

Above: In this picture of Egyptian mythology, the goddess of the sky, Nut, forms the canopy of the sky with her body, while the people below walk on the earth, which is really the god Geb. The figure with the outstretched arms is the goddess Shu, who separates the sky from the earth. **Opposite:** The soul of an Egyptian (dressed in white) waits while his heart is weighed on the scale before the god Osiris. The standing bird-headed figure is Thoth, the god of wisdom and writing, who is writing a transcript of the man's appeal. The jackal-headed god Anubis weighs the soul of the man against a tiny figure of the goddess Maat (the crouching figure on the scale). This canopic jar is unique because it has three compartments instead of the usual four.

traveling to Osiris' Realm or standing before this god of the dead in judgment come from the period of the New Kingdom.

However, not all of the literature from this period was practical or serious. A large amount of the literature produced at this time seems to have been devoted almost exclusively to entertainment, with complicated plots filled with magic, and all overlaid with a heavy emphasis on the gross, grotesque, and bawdy. *The Struggle Between Horus and Seth* is a rather crude story about the long-standing animosities between Horus, the son of Isis and Osiris, and his uncle, Seth. It was obviously written to appeal to a reader's worst imagination.

During these two gods' struggle for Osiris' throne after his death, Horus suffers the indignity of being raped from behind by Seth. However, Horus manages to catch Seth's semen in his hand before it can enter him and so—strange as it sounds to us—avoids the disgrace of being raped in the eyes of the ancient Egyptians. Later, Horus masturbates and secretly covers Seth's salad with his semen, then watches as his uncle eats the salad. When the two gods testify before a heavenly tribunal set up to determine

who should be king, Seth triumphantly claims he is superior because he has raped Horus. Horus denies the charge, and asks the gods to examine both himself and his uncle. When they do, they discover that Horus is free of semen but that Seth has Horus' semen in his stomach. The same story has Isis accidentally harpooning Horus in the eye, and Horus cutting off his mother's head. Altogether it is a bawdy parody of Egyptian religion with something to offend everyone.

Another story, *The Tale of Two Brothers*, involves a pair of brothers, Anubis and Bata, who have a falling out over Anubis' wife. She tries to seduce Bata, and when he rejects her she tells Anubis that Bata raped her. Anubis is furious, but Bata proclaims his innocence and proves it by slicing off his own penis, apparently demonstrating in the most graphic (and painful) way possible that he was not sexually interested in Anubis' wife. Anubis, realizing his mistake, bashes in his wife's head. Bata, feeling that he needs some time away from home, travels to Lebanon, where he magically gets a new penis and marries the daughter of a local king. The girl has the peculiarity of always smelling of a strong perfume that acts as an aphrodisiac. When an Egyptian merchant visits Lebanon, he tries to rape the girl, but she runs away. The merchant only manages to yank out a handful of her hair as she flees. On his return to Egypt, he shows this hair to the pharaoh, who, overcome by the perfume, sends rich presents to Lebanon to tempt the woman into leaving Bata. After one look at the jewelry the pharaoh has sent, the materialistic girl immediately goes to Egypt.

Bata follows, determined to get his wife back. In Egypt, he disguises himself as a bull. His faithless wife, however, recognizes him and persuades the pharaoh, who does not know who the bull really is, to sacrifice the animal. Just before the sacrifice, however,

Bata changes himself into two trees. The wife, who has anticipated this change, then persuades the pharaoh to cut down the trees. Bata, not to be outdone, changes himself into a berry on one of the trees, which falls into his wife's mouth. The berry makes the wife pregnant, and the wife gives birth to—of course—Bata. The pharaoh, believing that the child is his, decrees that on his death the man will become pharaoh. In time the pharaoh does die, and Bata becomes king, executes his wife-mother, and summons his long-lost brother Anubis to be his vizier. The brothers are thus reunited, and they rule Egypt wisely and well.

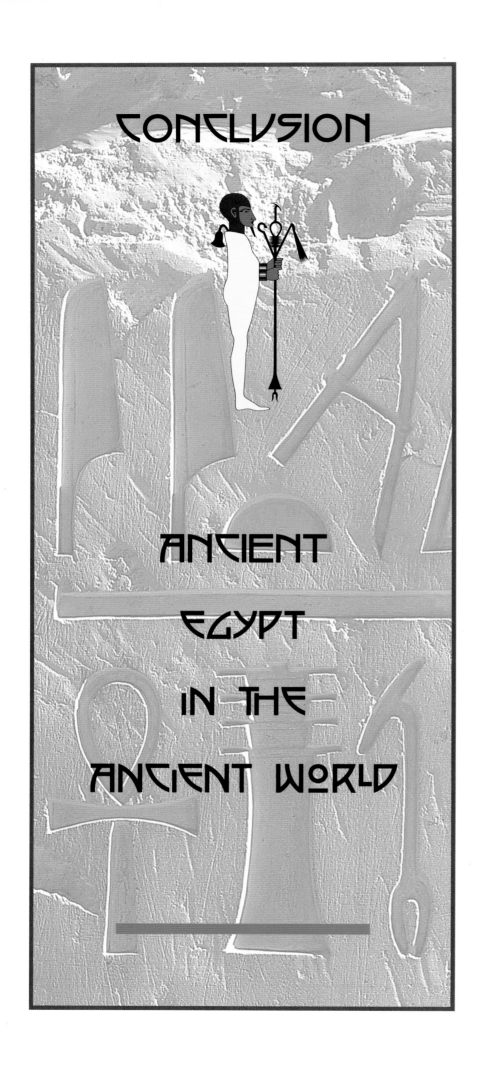

CONCLUSION

ANCIENT EGYPT IN THE ANCIENT WORLD

The New Kingdom period exemplified Egypt at its apex. Never again would Egypt stand so high in the regard of the rest of the world. But even after the empire was finally defeated and came to be dominated by other nations, something of its grandeur always remained.

Even her conquerors tried to clothe themselves in the glory of that ancient culture. The Nubians who came up from the south to conquer Egypt early in the eighth millennium grafted Egyptian culture wholesale onto their own. The ancient Greeks, who certainly created one of the greatest civilizations of the ancient world, looked upon Egypt as a source of much knowledge, science, even religion. When Alexander the Great conquered Egypt in 332 B.C., he felt compelled to participate in the glory of ancient Egypt by having himself crowned pharaoh. Even the Romans, who conquered Egypt in the first century B.C. and professed to be scandalized by the decadence of Cleopatra and her world, felt that Egypt was the crowning jewel in their Mediterranean Empire, and that political dominance over that mysterious eastern country somehow conferred on Rome an uncontested right to rule the world.

ANCIENT EGYPT
IN THE ANCIENT WORLD

BIBLIOGRAPHY

Aldred, Cyril. *The Egyptians.* Revised edition. London: Thames and Hudson, 1984.

Baines, John, and Jaromir Malek. *Atlas of Ancient Egypt.* New York: Facts on File, 1984.

David, A. Rosalie. *The Egyptian Kingdoms.* New York: Peter Bedrick, 1988.

——. *The Pyramid Builders of Ancient Egypt.* London and New York: Routledge, 1986.

Desroches-Noblecourt, Christiane. *Tutankhamen.* New York: New York Graphic Society, 1963.

Donadoni, Sergio, ed. *The Egyptians.* Chicago: University of Chicago Press, 1997.

Finegan, Jack. *Archaeological History of the Ancient Middle East.* New York: Barnes and Noble, 1979.

Guillemette, Andrea. *Egypt in the Age of the Pyramids.* Translated by David Lorton. Ithaca, New York: Cornell University Press, 1997.

Hoffman, Michael A. *Egypt Before the Pharaohs.* New York: Alfred A. Knopf, 1979.

Hornung, Erik. *Conceptions of God in Ancient Egypt.* Translated by John Baines. Ithaca, New York: Cornell University Press, 1971.

Hurry, Jamieson B. *Imhotep: The Egyptian God of Medicine.* Chicago: Ares, 1987.

James, T.G.H. *Ancient Egypt: The Land and the Legacy.* Austin: University of Texas Press, 1990.

Kemp, Barry J. *Ancient Egypt: Anatomy of a Civilization.* London: Routledge, 1989.

Meeks, Dimitri, and Christine Favard-Meeks. *Daily Life of the Egyptian Gods.* Translated by G. M. Goshgarian. Ithaca, New York: Cornell University Press, 1993.

Mendelssohn, Kurt. *The Riddle of the Pyramids.* New York: Praeger, 1974.

Nunn, John F. *Ancient Egyptian Medicine.* Norman: University of Oklahoma Press, 1996.

Roberts, Timothy R. *Ancient Civilizations.* New York: Smithmark, 1997.

Somers, Clark, and R. Engelbach. *Ancient Egyptian Construction and Architecture.* Mineola, New York: Dover, 1990.

Trigger, Bruce G. *Early Civilizations: Ancient Egypt in Context.* Cairo, Egypt: American University of Cairo Press, 1993.

Tyldesley, Joyce. *Hatchepsut: The Female Pharaoh.* London: Viking, Penguin, 1996.

INDEX

PHOTO CREDITS